The White Trash Mom
HANDBOOK

Embrace Your Inner Trailerpark,

Forget Perfection, Resist Assimilation

into the PTA, Stay Sane, and

Keep Your Sense of Humor

The White Trash Mom
HANDBOOK

MICHELLE LAMAR

with

MOLLY WENDLAND

ST. MARTIN'S GRIFFIN 🜲 NEW YORK

www.stmartins.com

Book design by Ellen Cipriano

LIBRARY OF CONGRESS CATALOGING-IN-PUBLICATION DATA

Lamar, Michelle.
  The white trash mom handbook : embrace your inner trailerpark, forget perfection, resist assimilation into the PTA, stay sane, and keep your sense of humor / Michelle Lamar, with Molly Wendland.—1st ed.
      p.   cm.
  ISBN-13: 978-0-312-37122-7
  ISBN-10: 0-312-37122-5
  1. Motherhood—United States—Humor.   2. Mothers—United States—Humor.   I. Wendland, Molly.   II. Title.
  HQ759.L335 2008
  306.874'30207—dc22   2008013012

First Edition: August 2008

10 9 8 7 6 5 4 3 2 1

To Grace and Kate with love.
Someday you'll have children of your own,
and I want a front-row seat.

To my husband, Tim, for
his infinite patience, love, and cooking abilities.

Contents

Acknowledgments ix

Preface: Why Perfection Is Overrated xi

1. Everyone Has a Little WT Inside 1

2. Are You a White Trash Mom? 9

3. Every Mother Is a Working Mother 23

4. The Zen of the White Trash Mom 33

5. School Talk 48

6. The Muffia 57

7. School Volunteerism and Your "ROI" 72

8. Fakin' It for the Bake Sale 92

9. After-School Activities for the White
Trash Family 103

10. Your Children *Will* Be in Therapy . . . Get
Used to It 117

11. "Commando Is Good for You" and Other
White Trash Lies You Tell Your Kids 131

12. If the Health Department Isn't Coming,
It's Clean Enough 144

13. Boring Summer Vacations (and Other Ways
I Deprive My Kids) 163

14. At the End of the Day 174

Appendix A The White Trash Mom's Hall of Fame 177

Appendix B The White Trash Mom's Bookshelf 189

Appendix C The White Trash Mom at the Movies 193

Appendix D Cookin' with the White Trash Mom 195

Appendix E The White Trash Mom's Favorite
Blogs and Web Sites 203

Appendix F The White Trash Mom's Frequently
Asked Questions 207

The White Trash Mom Glossary 211

Acknowledgments

First, I want to thank my agent and friend Stephanie Kip Rostan from Levine-Greenberg for taking a chance on a book called *The White Trash Mom Handbook*. Thanks, Stephanie, for seeing my idea and making it a reality. It couldn't have happened without you. Thanks also to Monica Verma, who is smart, wonderful, and has a great perspective. Second, thank you to Sheila Curry Oakes, my wonderful and savvy editor at St. Martin's Press, for taking my manuscript and making it a book. Sheila, I appreciate your patience and I am fortunate to work with you. Alyse Diamond at St. Martin's Press is a dream. Thanks, Alyse, for all you do.

My family is awesome and I don't know what I would do without Jill, Mark, Connor, Melinda, and my man Ward. Thank you, Troester family, for adopting all of us and making us part of your awesome group. I am lucky to have a wonderful family on my husband's side, especially Patricia, my incredible mother-in-law.

I consider some women my family, even though we don't share any DNA. Katie, Nancy, MariAnn, CeCe, Laura, Missy, Tracey,

Kate B., and Molly are all in my personal WT Mom Hall of Fame and I don't know what I would do without you. I wish every mother could have a group like the Wichita Mafia to get support, laughs, and when needed, a kick in the rear. Thanks to Jill, Mary, Polly, Ruth, Becker, Anne, Cath, and Kelly. Your advice and friendship mean the world to me. Thanks to some other special women who I include as part of my "Mafia" but don't see enough, like Gina, Amy, Jen, Jody, Jan, Barb, Deb, Martha, Kristen, and Tracy. JoAnn, I'm glad you are back in my life and your encouragement is invaluable. Thanks to my school angels, Carolyn, Donna, Maura, Kathleen, Maureen, and Diane, for having the grace to deal with a White Trash Mom. I would be lost in the sea of school paperwork without Cindy, Kristen, and Barb.

I wish every working mom could have clients and mentors like Jim, Kristen Marie, Gigi, Glo, Tanya, and Bill. The world would be a better and more balanced place for families if every mom could work with you guys. I am grateful for the amazing people at Disney Interactive and my editors. You gave White Trash Mom a chance when other companies would not.

Thanks to the wise and loving women who mothered me for years, especially after I lost my own dear mother. I appreciate the love and support from my aunties; I am thankful to Sally and Nancy W. for taking me under their wing.

I have a long list of other writers and bloggers that are my daily support and provide hours of laughter. I've listed a bunch of blogs in the back of the book and I'm sure I left out some.

Finally, thank you, Molly Wendland, Tacky Princess, for your patience, your keen eye, your creativity, and just being you. You complete my trailerpark.

Preface

Why Perfection Is Overrated

Modern mothers are expected to look like Heather Locklear and pull down a six-figure salary while home schooling the kids. This standard of perfection is the status quo in today's culture.

I began writing a blog in August 2005 as a way of dealing with some of the ridiculous and insane expectations that are part of modern motherhood. I called my blog White Trash Mom. I gave it a trashy name and wrote about my life with a snarky and humorous tone. As soon as I started the blog, the floodgates opened. I heard from women all over the United States and the world, and many women identified with me and told me their experiences of living up to perfect expectations. I can't tell you how many times I hear *I thought I was the only one who felt that way* or *I thought I was the only one who thought that was wrong.*

I was not alone. You are not alone. Mothers have to stick together in the face of outrageous ideas of how we should look, behave, and live. The current state of motherhood isn't going to change overnight. Your kids will be grown by the time real change occurs. But because things aren't going to change any time soon, my book is an attempt to offer some ideas and shortcuts to make the wait time more pleasurable.

Fight the Insanity with the Right Weapons

Mothers are expected to do the impossible on a daily basis, wearing six-inch pumps and a thong. The expectations are insane and moms can't win that battle. Since the mothers are set up to fail, I believe we should fight back by whatever methods we can. We *can't* play by the rules because the rules, in the words of my teenager . . . *suck*. That's where White Trash Mom comes in.

"White Trash" Is a State of Mind

There are a lot of crazy ideas about what makes a good mother these days. If you don't have a body like a movie star, pull down a big salary, dress like a sex kitten, and home school your kids, you are a loser. You are a failure if you are not a super-mom. In fact, trying to be the perfect mom can only drive you crazy.

Once you admit to yourself how ridiculous some of the expectations for moms are, you can begin to change your attitude and become what I like to call a White Trash Mom.

No Trailerpark Necessary

A White Trash Mom doesn't have to be white or trashy or live in a double-wide down by the river. It has nothing to do with socio-economic status.

A White Trash Mom represents a philosophy and a perspective

on motherhood. Being a lifelong smart-ass, I gave this philosophy of parenting a smart-ass name.

It's a name I chose to represent the opposite of perfection. Perfect is in . . . so if you're not a perfect mom, you're a White Trash Mom.

This book is an attempt to help you find your perspective on motherhood. Navigate your own shortcuts through the insane expectations. You can call your philosophy "Yankee Fabulous" or "Santa Monica Slacker." Call it whatever you want but find a way to work around the rules.

Why I Became a White Trash Mom

It was not my lifelong goal to become known as White Trash Mom. I began writing about white trash motherhood in protest against the onslaught of "shoulds" and "musts" we moms face every day. We all know these expectations are unrealistic, but we can't help but hold ourselves up against them and become discouraged when we can't measure up. We know it's propaganda but it can still make us feel just a teeny bit inferior. We have encountered these unrealistic expectations in the media, our neighborhoods, and homes.

Mothers Who Look Like Supermodels

We *know* that the sixteen-year-old models who weigh seventy-nine pounds and are featured in the magazine ads for "mommy and me" clothes are not really *moms*. We know that they are models and actresses, and are some art director's hallucination (albeit a concentration-camp type of hallucination) of what a mom should look like. We know all the photos in the magazines are airbrushed. But we can't help it; we still compare ourselves.

Quick and Easy Is Neither

We know that Martha Stewart and others like her have a staff of forty to do the cucumber sandwiches for that magazine article that features Martha and her "easy cucumber sandwiches." We know that much of what is pitched to moms in the media is propaganda and is not real. Deep inside, you doubt yourself just a little when you read that article about the "easy cucumber sandwiches," and don't make them for your next luncheon or tea. Never mind that your last "luncheon" was eaten in the car on the way to little Susie's soccer practice.

Myth of Perfection

So, know that the myth of perfection is a scam. But hardly anyone writes about it or talks about it. Every mother buys into the "ideal" and spends the first few years of her mom career beating herself up for not measuring up. It doesn't feel right and doesn't do much for the old self-esteem but because we think that we're the only one—we don't fight the system.

Good News . . . You Are Not Alone

You're not a bad mother if the school has to call you because your kid has a negative balance for his school lunch account. You're not a bad mother if your kid is the last one picked up from school. You aren't the only one who feels like you are a bad mom if you don't have your kids signed up for ten different sports and a language class (or two). Lots of moms feel pressure to look like a "sex kitten," wear chic clothes while pulling down a full-time job and heading up the PTA. Even when you figure out that it's impossible to "do it all," you've wasted years of your life trying to shoehorn yourself into a role that just doesn't fit. If you're lucky, you find other moms like you who know perfection is overrated and together you discover that the way to deal with motherhood is to have some great friends, a good sense of humor, and a taste for adventure.

Finding Your Inner White Trash Mom

Because the modern standard of perfection for mothers is not going away overnight, you have to play along with the charade to a certain degree. Sometimes you can buck the system but it can be a lot easier to play along. But you don't have to lose your soul, or your sense of humor, in the process. I am going to reveal some of my White Trash Mom secrets, so that reality and sanity can become a regular part of your daily life.

There are times you have to confront the problems head on but you have to work within the current "system" most of the time. You have to play the game but that doesn't mean that you can't play along by some of your own rules!

This book is a guide to help you find your own White Trash methods of cheating the system. I want to help you find your inner White Trash Mom so that reality and sanity can creep back into your daily life.

The White Trash Mom philosophy is catching on and I am hopeful that we can eventually change the world . . . one mom at a time.

Please keep these things in mind as you read this book:

It's okay to lie . . . sometimes.

Some of my tactics involve being dishonest. For example, pretending that you baked a cake when you really bought it at the store. I don't think lying is the right way to live your life. But extreme situations sometimes call for extreme solutions. The only reason I give the advice I do is because the current expectations of motherhood are so unrealistic. Call fudging your culinary skills the lesser of two evils.

My backyard is a lot like yours.

The problems and issues that are discussed in this book are universal. Just because I write about issues in my children's school or our church doesn't mean it's a criticism of one community or school. It's just a way of showing you that what happens here can happen anywhere. And believe me, it does.

Find your inner trailerpark.

This book is more of an idea grab bag for coping with kids, school, and more without losing your mind or your sense of humor.

Preschool is the pregame.

There are tons of baby books and books that tell you how to balance work and motherhood. Many of these books concentrate on the days when children are newborn to age four. It's only after your kids are old enough to trust them not to stick a fork in the electrical outlet or drink toilet water that the *tough part* of your job as a mom begins. The baby and toddler years are the pregame, ladies. Elementary school is where "the big show" begins and you need to combine the diplomatic skills of a UN ambassador with the quick-change skills of a Las Vegas showgirl to be on the front lines of the battlefield.

The White Trash Mom
HANDBOOK

Everyone Has a
Little WT Inside

Many educated people say they don't watch TV. Alternatively, they watch TV but say they only watch "PBS documentaries or news." If this is true, then why is *American Idol* the highest-rated TV show on the planet? More Americans vote for their favorite singer on *American Idol* than vote for president. People pretend they are perfect but everyone has a little WT inside. Nowhere is the myth of perfection more dramatic than in the sacred area of *motherhood*.

PERFECT VERSUS WHITE TRASH

The message to mothers is that you must have the cool career and the family and the size-zero figure. The message all of us in the motherhood trenches hear all the time is that *it's easy to do it all*. Nobody seems to mention that a woman "doing it all" is a movie star who is a working mom but also has a full-time nanny, a cook, a personal trainer, and a driver.

Mere mortals read the articles about high-profile moms and beat themselves up over the fact they cannot juggle the career and family with the same ease that is depicted in the magazines and on TV. Many women know in their heads that much of the stuff they read is propaganda but there is just so much of it that most modern moms have doubts about their inability to do it "all." Being a White Trash Mom is the answer.

THE WHITE TRASH MOM PHILOSOPHY

Trust Yourself

My definition of a White Trash Mom is a mother who is true to her own values. A mother who does not completely give in to the pressures of what other people think when raising her kids. You have to listen to your gut *but work within the system* to be able to raise a family that has the kind of values you want them to have.

Work Around the Rules

There is a "system" in place, at every school in America, for what the "perfect" mother is. It is part of every school's hidden curriculum. If you are too much of a rebel and try to buck this system, it is your child who pays the price. The insane standards for perfection aren't going away while your kids are in school. So you need to find your own shortcuts to work within the system while raising your kids in a sane way. Find the "cheats" that will allow you to participate without losing your mind.

Laugh

A sense of humor about motherhood goes a long way. There is nowhere in the world where mom pressure is felt more than in elementary schools, middle schools, and high schools. And you thought playground politics were over once you got out of school. Think again. It's worse than the junior high lunchroom.

PART OF YOUR JOB AS A MOTHER IS TO PLAY THE GAME

Starting in elementary school, part of your job as a parent is to work with the school and the other parents. You can balk, make fun, and rebel against this expectation—but your child will be labeled for it and it will make it a tougher road for them in school and with friends.

It is possible to keep your eye on the values *you* want to raise your kids with while participating in some of the insanity that is expected of modern parents. I wanted to make a road map for myself and other moms like me that think some modern parenting "norms" are not normal at all.

This book will help you figure out how to work within the "system" you are living in without sacrificing your core values. You have to figure out the rules and the "system" at your child's school and then figure out how to work around some of the rules while still working within the system at times. Again, if you completely rebel, it is your child who pays the price, not you. I'm not making this stuff up!

THE HIDDEN CURRICULUM

A very smart man named Richard Lavoie gave me a name for the "system" that faces every student and every family at their school. The hidden curriculum is different at every school and unique to each school culture. Lavoie puts it best when he says, "Like snowflakes, no two are alike."

Lavoie did not create the term *hidden curriculum*; it comes from a study of school cultures done in 1986. The study revealed the enormous power of these unwritten rules:

- ❖ The hidden curriculum impacts the performance, productivity, progress, and attitudes of the every student at the school.
- ❖ The hidden curriculum is created, maintained, and manipulated by the students and staff of every school.
- ❖ The hidden curriculum is both constructive and destructive in nature.
- ❖ Changes to the hidden curriculum are slow and laborious, and innovations are often viewed skeptically. The skepticism can border on paranoia.

All this hidden curriculum stuff applies to moms as well. You need to become aware of the unspoken rules at your child's school and you need to try to blend in with the system. You don't have to become a phony, but remember, at the end of the day you are doing it all for your kids.

Here's the Truth that Nobody Else Is Telling You

You need to learn the rules and play the game if you want to give your child the best chance of success at school. You don't have to be PTA president or volunteer every day—but you have to find a way to be involved in the system for your child. You don't have to love it but you have to do it. Don't make me get out my ruler from Catholic school. Just put on your big-girl panties and deal with it! Before you think I'm going to turn you into a soccer mom instead of a White Trash Mom, read on to learn how it starts to get tricky—and fun!

Why You Need a White Trash Mom

As much as you might not want to hear what I have to say, you need to listen. It's a crazed world out there. Who are you going to ask about this stuff? Your mom? If you are lucky enough to have your mother around, she is probably not much help because when you were a kid they didn't have so many activities. There were no cell phones or MySpace.com. Depending on your age, your mom probably told you to "be home before dinner" and made herself a cocktail at 4 P.M. I'm not pining away for the "good old days." I'm just saying your mom's advice will only get you so far. Or *Dr. Wonderman's Book of Childhood*. I'm sure it's my own insecurities but I hate to read parenting books by doctors and professionals. Some of the best advice you can get about modern parenting is going to come from those in the trenches of motherhood. *The White Trash Mom Handbook* shows you how to find the people who share your values about parenting.

Most Moms Don't Want to Talk About It

Most moms don't want to admit that they stayed up until 3 A.M. to get the cookies for the bake sale done or that the chairwoman of their school committee scares them to death. The expectations for motherhood are crazy but most mothers think *all the other moms* are balancing things just fine, so they keep quiet. White Trash Mom wants to bring all the insanity into the open.

The White Trash Mom Rules for Sanity

The perfect mother does not exist.
There is no such thing as the perfect mother. Besides that, perfection is overrated.

You have to play the game.
You have to play the game . . . but there are ways to "cheat" and find loopholes of sanity.

You will screw up your kids.
You are going to make mistakes with your kids. Your children will be in therapy. It's just a matter of when and for how long.

Trust YOUR instincts.
Your neurotic quirks are just as good as any child psychologist's. Trust your own instincts and let your own neurotic tendencies mess up your kids.

Motherhood is not a spectator sport.
You aren't parenting for show. You are trying to raise little humans into big humans. Do what is best for your kid and your family.

Do what works for you.
I'm not saying my way is the right way. I'm saying this is what worked for me and this book will show you how to find what will work for you.

Success is a moving target.
Trying to juggle work, life, and children is like hitting a moving target. Once you find what works for you, you need to be able to adapt the plan as the needs of the family change.

LETTER TO THE "PERFECT MOTHERS" FROM WHITE TRASH MOM

Perfection is everywhere. It seems like some of the mothers you meet or read about can "do it all" without breaking a sweat. I'm tired of being made to feel lousy because I can't juggle the jobs of three adults at the same time. Here's what I'd like to say to all of the "perfect mothers" and all the companies that help feed the myth of the "perfect mother":

Dear Perfect Mothers,

It upsets me because so many mothers look at you and then berate themselves for not being able to do it "all." I believe women should support other women but I have to tell you: **Please stop the madness!** *You are* contributing to a major problem in our culture by pretending to be perfect. I have a few questions for you about how you "do it all":

- How many people do you have on staff in your home?
- How many maids?
- How many nannies?
- Are your kids really your kids? Or are they actors? I am suspicious of any mom who says the kids clean up after themselves.
- Does your husband actually help?
- Do you have actual proof of your husband helping you? Documentation?
- Is your husband, in fact, a robot?
- If he is not a robot, where can I get one?
- Do you sleep at night? Or do you just walk the earth like the undead?
- What drugs are you taking to make you so efficient, and can I have some?
- Are you, in fact, an alien?
- If you really are doing it all, without drugs or supernatural powers, would you please make a video/book for the rest of us?

I know women can work outside the home and have a family. But juggling a job and motherhood isn't pretty. It's sure not easy.

Being a mother is a full-time job all by itself, so please tell us how you juggle it. **Cut it out and give us the real story, perfect moms.** Because the myth that women can do it "all" and that doing it all is easy is a story that brings all of us down.

Cheers,
White Trash Mom

Strap on your white-trash apron, kick-start your sense of humor, and let's begin to unleash your inner WT mom.

2

Are You a
White Trash Mom?

Before we go any farther, it's time to take a little test. Let's face it. You wouldn't have bought this book if you didn't have a little bit of a trashy side. Take this quiz and find out just how deep in the trailerpark you are.

PART I   WHITE TRASH MOM QUIZ

Drive-Through Etiquette

1. You have used a credit card at a fast-food drive-up window.

2. You have used a credit card at a fast-food drive-up window *for less than $3.00.*

3. You have never used cash at a fast-food drive-up window.

Home Cooking

1. The local pizza delivery joint immediately knows your name and address.
2. The local pizza delivery joint recognizes your voice when you call to order.
3. The pizza delivery guy exchanges Christmas cards with your family.

Food Groups

1. Your kids get excited when you purchase cheese in a can.
2. Your kids believe Velveeta is cheese, not cheese food.
3. Your kids think all cheese is cheese in a can.

Tooth Fairy

1. You never forget the tooth fairy.
2. You forget to put money under the pillow the night the tooth comes out, but you put in an extra buck when you do it the next night.
3. You forget about the tooth fairy for a week—and put $20 under the pillow when you remember.

Sucking Up to Teachers (Little Susie's teacher has a birthday.)

1. You do nothing.
2. You send the teacher a nice birthday card.
3. You give the teacher a gift certificate to a local nail salon for a mani.

Medication and You (The school psychologist tells you your kid has ADD.)
1. You get a second opinion.
2. You take the kid to a shrink who writes *both of you* an Adderall prescription.
3. You go to a shrink who writes your kid an Adderall prescription. You take the Adderall and make the kid play outside more.

Shopping Smarts (The annual shoe sale at Nordstrom's is one day only.)
1. You take your preteen daughter after school.
2. You pick her up early from school to go.
3. You call her in sick to school and you shop all day.

Working and You (Your new supervisor is a stickler for people staying past 5 P.M.)
1. You stay past 5 P.M. to win him over.
2. You try to negotiate with him for flextime.
3. You purchase an additional purse, which you leave in your cube. You leave early but leave the desk light on, and keep your desk messy so everyone thinks you are still there.

Communicating with Your Offspring (When you walk into your eight-year-old's room, which of the phrases below sounds like you?)
1. "Thank you, Todd, for cleaning up your room like you promised."

2. "This room is a pigsty . . . I mean it. You have got to clean this up."
3. "Jesus, Mary, and Joseph! Were you raised in a *barn?*"

Training Your Offspring (You trained your offspring at an early age to do the following:)
1. Clear the dishes from the dinner table.
2. Bring you beers from the refrigerator.
3. Mix a smooth margarita on the rocks with a touch of salt around the glass.

Culture in Your Household (What is your idea of the arts?)
1. Your children don't watch anything but PBS.
2. Your kids think there are two kinds of music: Country . . . and Western.
3. Your kids learned the words to "Goodbye Earl" by the Dixie Chicks in preschool.

Hair Color (What is the appropriate age for a girl to get highlights in her hair?)
1. Never. Be happy with the hair God gave you.
2. Highlights are fine for high school girls and older.
3. If she makes it out of third grade without a highlight, she'll be the first one in your family.

Training Female Offspring for the Real World (Your ten-year-old is able to spot the following from a distance:)
1. The blue-spotted hoot owl.
2. A cop using his radar gun at cars.
3. Which celebrity has recently undergone plastic surgery (and name the procedure).

Training Male Offspring for the Real World (Your
   ten-year-old is trained to spot the following from
   a distance:)
   1. The blue-spotted hoot owl.
   2. The liquor store.
   3. The closest Hooters restaurant.

HOW TO SCORE FOR PART I
   ❖ Give yourself zero points for every time you picked
      number 1.
   ❖ Give yourself one point for every number 2 answer.
   ❖ Give yourself two points for every number 3 answer.

SCORE OF 0–5
Clearly you have picked up the wrong book. You are looking for
a book called *How to Get Your Laundry White* or *How to Organize
Your Trash into Craft Items.* You have not yet awakened to your
trashy side.

SCORE OF 5–10
You are one generation removed from the trailerpark.
   You've got a nice amount of trashy in you and you are
probably on the younger side of motherhood or you are still
getting in touch with your inner WT Mom. Stay awhile, my
friend. Read up on the shortcuts of being a WT Mom. I think
you will see the light.

SCORE OF 10–20 OR
YOU DIDN'T EVEN TAKE THE QUIZ
You are already there. You can take the girl outta Wichita but you
can't take the Wichita outta the girl. Sister, you may live in a

million-dollar subdivision but you can't hide from your WT destiny.
You're a card-carrying member of the White Trash Mom's club.

PART II   WHITE TRASH MOM QUIZ (ANSWER YES OR NO TO THE FOLLOWING QUESTIONS.)

- ❖ My children call soda pop "kid beers."
- ❖ My children lie on the phone and tell people I'm asleep if someone calls during *American Idol* or *Project Runway*.
- ❖ My children think the word "shit" is a normal part of daily conversation.
- ❖ My third-grader's favorite TV show is *The O.C.* reruns.
- ❖ My children can quote most of the dialogue for *Talladega Nights: The Ballad of Ricky Bobby*.
- ❖ My children call a scotch and water "mommy's juice."
- ❖ My children learned to order pizza delivery by age seven.
- ❖ My children think the dog's name is "that damn dog."
- ❖ My children have gotten angry with me for borrowing cash from them.
- ❖ My child picked the name of an alcoholic beverage for a camp name.[1]
- ❖ My child knows what celebrities have had plastic surgery. Example: "Jane Doe Celebrity has definitely gotten some work done."[2]
- ❖ My child reads *People* magazine more than once a year.

1. These are real incidents in a White Trash Mom's life. I can't make this stuff up.
2. Ibid.

HOW TO SCORE FOR PART II

If you answered "yes" to any of these questions, you have significant WTM traits. You are on your way to being a White Trash Mom.

Other Ways to Know If You're a WT Mom

If you don't "test well" on the White Trash Mom quiz or you are too lazy to take the WTM quiz, here are some additional signs you may be well on the road to WT motherhood.

Pretending "It Just Happened"

You pretend that the rip in your jeans or the stain on your shirt *just happened.* Even though the stain/rip/tear has been there for two years and you just keep forgetting to do something about it.

You Laugh More Than Other Moms You Know

Being a mother means being completely insane some of the time. Dealing with a kid on a regular basis is, by its very nature, a cause for crazy behavior. It's wonderful but you have to admit it is a little ridiculous that a grown woman needs to remember that the purple Teletubby is the one with the purse *or* that you have to watch the latest YouTube video with your eleven-year-old again and again. A White Trash Mom laughs at the odd parts of motherhood; she has her sense of humor intact.

"Only at Home" Rule

You find yourself telling the kids not to brag that you let them watch the new violent movie that just came out because you know the other parents probably would not approve. You make sure your first-grader understands that when she plays the game where she "gets Daddy a beer" that it's a game only to be played *at home*, as you don't want to get a visit from Child Services.

You've Sent Your Kids to School with No Lunch or No Socks or Some Offense that "Other Moms" Don't Do

You could be on the road to WTMville if you have ever forgotten to give your kids their lunch or they go to school with no socks because all the socks are in the wash. Or you were the last one to pick up your kid, because you forgot they got out early that day. I'm not saying you do this every day; your White Trash Mom status means you have forgotten something really *basic*. The bonus is that your child will remind you about the thing you forgot for the next twenty years.

You've Experienced One of the Big D's in Life— Death, Divorce

There is nothing like a major life crisis to give a person perspective.

If someone you love has died or you have lived through the hell of divorce (as a child or as an adult) you can see how quickly life can shift. Losses like this can give people a new perspective and often let them rely on their own values and instincts rather than worrying about people around you and what they think.

FINDING OTHER WHITE TRASH MOMS

Once you know you are WT, then you need to find one of your own to help navigate and negotiate the elementary school jungle.

During the culture shock of my daughter's kindergarten year, I was a fish out of water. I turned to some of my veteran mom pals, who had older children, for support. Unfortunately, neither of my friends had children my daughter's age but I relied on them to help me figure out the hidden culture of my daughter's class.

> **VETS:** Get your school directory.
> **ME:** My what?
> **VETS:** The damn school directory, woman! It's the bible.
> **ME:** The white book they gave us the first day of school?
> **VETS:** (Disgusted silence)

After I found the directory in my linen closet, we began the conference call. We went through the names of most of the moms who were in my daughter's class at school, some of whom had older kids and were known to my friends. At the end of the call, there was a breakthrough.

> **VETS:** This grade does have a lot of "Muffia" activity. It's a tough situation.
> **ME:** Is there any hope?
> **VET #1:** Lucky for you that my cousin has kids in this grade.

Through this phone call, I found one of my best friends in the world. This woman has been a mentor, supporter, and true-blue friend ever since. We've been through a lot together and we'll be lifelong friends.

Spotting the White Trash Mom in Her Native Habitat

If you don't know anyone at your school and need to find a fellow WTM, here's what to look for. This task is harder than it sounds because a WTM is a rebel underground of mothers. Just because the mom wears ripped jeans doesn't mean she's one of us.

You have to look for the subtle clues to find one of our own. Here are a few tips on what to look for when trying to find another member of the WTM underground:

A Good Laugh

A percentage of the WTM population can be identified by a hearty laugh. A woman might look like she stepped out of a Talbot's catalog but a deep and hearty laugh is usually a sign of WTM potential. If you are at a parent meeting or school play and something funny happens, you will hear one or two women in the crowd with a hearty "guffaw" of laughter. Go find the woman in question after the school event and keep an eye on this woman. A woman who has a vigorous laugh is a good candidate for the White Trash Mom list. A sense of humor is invaluable in a friend and ally, especially among White Trash Moms.

The Eyes Have It

The eyes are the windows to the soul . . . and a clue to possible WTM friends. The typical WTM has bright eyes that make contact with you when you speak. True White Trash Mom's eyes don't wander off, looking above you or through you for a more desirable person to socialize with.

The Lunch or Coffee Test

WTMs are not snobs. Our underground movement is not about being superior. If you suspect another mom might have WTM potential, invite her for coffee or lunch. You can tell a lot about a person by how they treat a waitress or the guy behind the Starbucks counter.

Accessories as Signs of the Home Team

Accessories are often a hidden sign to other WTMs that you are on the same team. A mom might look like she's straight out of the *Stepford Wives* movie but if you notice that she always wears crazy shoes, she may be a White Trash Mom. You might see a mom you think is no way part of the sisterhood but then you notice she's carrying a *funked-out* purse . . . with lots of paper and stuff overflowing. There's a WTM in there somewhere.

Example: I spotted one of my future best friends at a school function because I noticed that she carried a funky purse made out of soda-pop cans. This woman dresses in classic preppy fashion but I saw she was carrying that purse so I struck up a conversation with her and later found that she is a complete WT Mom.

The "Walks Like a Duck" Rule

My dad always said: If it looks like a duck, walks like a duck, and smells like a duck . . . it's a duck.
Translation: *Trust* your instincts.

EMBRACE YOUR INNER WHITE TRASH MOM

Being a White Trash Mom means that there is in you still a bit of the person you were before you became a mom. Being a mother means changing your focus. So much of your energy goes into raising and nurturing your kids and isn't focused on yourself.

Key Differences in Being a White Trash Mom

WT Moms still hold on to a flicker of that light they had before they had kids. They can still laugh about some of the same things, still remember who they were before they were mothers. This is a key difference between White Trash Moms and other moms. Motherhood can engulf a woman. She can turn herself over completely to her kids. I'm not recommending neglecting the kids but you can't let the kids take over your life and personality. You have to juggle the part of you that is an individual with the *you* that is a mom.

You can allow your "premom" self to shine through in small ways every day. Here are a few examples:

ACTIVITY	WHITE TRASH MOM	NORMAL MOM
Car tunes for your duties as a chauffeur	"Best of the Eighties" sound track or other music from your life	Annoying kiddie sound tracks
Mother-child bonding	Manicure at the strip mall	Mommy-and-me cooking classes
Family game night	Poker	*Candy Land*

I believe that many women shift their focus *too much* away from who they were before they had children—these women become what they think they should be as a mother. . . . they become what they think is the "perfect mother."

Some women become mothers and they lose any glimmer of who they were before they had kids. There is no evidence of the "premom" person inside or, if the "premom" person *is* in there, that woman is hiding in the witness protection program.

Perfect is stupid and impossible. You can be a good mom without being perfect; you just have to be willing to try.

3

Every Mother Is
a Working Mother

There was a time when I still believed I could "do it all." I worked and worked and tried and tried and, of course, failed at being a perfect mother, wife, and executive.

I berated myself for wondering *why* I could not get it all done. I had a small child and a baby. I had a mother with cancer. I had to travel for work. My husband traveled for work. I know it sounds like I am about to whine but please read on. I promise I am making a point.

One day I woke up and realized that it was completely insane to try to think I could do it all. Something had to give. In my case, I had to get creative with the truth.

Ordinarily I think being straightforward and truthful is the way to go. But desperate times call for desperate measures. Why, you ask, did I need to go to such extremes? Because, campers, the working world is not set up for mothers.

We are on our own out there.

❖ Two-thirds of employed mothers do not have enough job flexibility to meet their caring and personal needs.

❖ Seventy percent of moms with children under eighteen work. A recent study by Harvard and McGill Universities ranks the United States at the bottom of the world's nations in terms of providing a safety net for moms and children.

❖ Of the 52 million working parents in the United States, it is estimated that $50 billion to $300 billion is dissipated annually in lost job productivity due to parents being worried and stressed about their children in after-school care or without proper after-school supervision.

Short of cloning yourself, you have to figure out ways to be where you need to be and try to make life work for your family. The situation modern mothers find themselves in is crazy. So I have some "innovative" ways to handle some of the situations you will find yourself in as you balance work and family.

WHITE TRASH MOM'S FAKE PURSE ESCAPE

If you work in an office situation, there are coworkers and/or supervisors who love to take note of when you arrive and when you leave the office.

It doesn't matter to these people how you perform or what work you get done during the day. It doesn't matter if you could still do some of this work at home via computer.

If you are faced with people who love to keep track of who

comes in late and leaves early, use my tried and true "fake purse" idea.

1. Buy an additional purse to keep in your desk.
2. If you need to leave before the stroke of 5 P.M. to get your children or to take someone to the doctor, leave the fake purse on your desk or hanging on your chair.
3. Have your desk a little messy and leave your desk light on. You want it to look like you are in the restroom and you'll be right back.

This is an excellent way to leave work early without the time-clock watchers taking note. Please know the "purse" ploy is very effective for when you need to leave a half-hour early but doesn't work for longer spans of time. For that you need a solution with a little more imagination.

WHITE TRASH MOM'S IMAGINARY CLIENT

When I was in sales, I found it easier to do doctors' appointments and kid activities because my job was based on performance and not on when I was at my desk. However, as a salesperson, you must account for your sales calls.

What was my WT solution? I made up a fake client. It made it easier for me to keep track of my excuses (lying is much more difficult than telling the truth) and it became a "code" for my coworkers (the women, of course) that I was on a "child duty" when I left the office.

I would tell my coworkers that I was going to see "Charlie" over at "Corporate Solutions" for a meeting.

At the mention of Charlie or a Corporate Solutions meeting, my friends would know that one of the girls had to go to the doctor or that I had playground duty at school.

This code also kept them alert so if a problem came up while I was at Charlie's, they could call me on my cell. I can't tell you how many work problems I took care of while on playground duty at my kids' school. It was hilarious.

WHITE TRASH MOM'S SUGGESTIONS FOR NONOFFICE JOBS

I've always worked office jobs since I've been a mom. If your work takes place in a store, a hospital, or a restaurant you can still "fake it till you make it." You simply have to get more creative.

Become the Homecoming Queen of Your Coworkers

If your work is "shift" based, like nurses, retail, and restaurant workers, your first mission is to immediately start campaigning to become the most beloved and popular worker on your shift. The Homecoming Queen, if you will, of your coworkers. Here are some ideas for how to become popular with coworkers:

❖ Volunteer to take their shifts when you can.
❖ Remember everyone's birthdays.
❖ Volunteer for the icky, boring paperwork project nobody wants to do.
❖ Bring cookies to work.

If you wage a campaign of kindness on your coworkers, you will benefit in the long run because you will build up good will—

"brownie points"—with the others. This is a key factor in the life of a working mom because you never know when child emergencies or school obligations will force you to look for help. If people love you, they will stand in line to help you when your child is sick or it's the day of the school play.

The Keeper of Schedules Is Your Best Friend

In addition to making your coworkers adore you, you must make sure the person in charge of creating the monthly/weekly schedule is on your side. You don't want to be a complete "brown-noser" because that will cause the other employees to distrust you. Gaining the trust and admiration of the one in charge of the schedule will benefit you (and your family) in the long run. Build up brownie points for that rainy day.

Sick Days

It is a given that your child will get sick on a day you have a big meeting or a day you have an important interview or conference call. For years, we had a nanny because of all the travel and irregular hours of my work and my husband's. We paid a small fortune to the nannies over the years. I would do it again in a heartbeat, as it was the best option for our family at that time. I work from home now and don't have a nanny. When my kids get sick or I have to juggle family and work, it can be interesting. I've written about some of my "juggling" experiences on my blog. I always get a huge response from readers on this topic because most mothers are doing the same thing I am, trying to make family and job demands work.

I have made conference calls in a closet. I have locked myself in a bathroom or been a part of a conference call while in my car, sitting in the driveway. For many businesses, it's not acceptable or professional to work from home. Your credibility is in question if you are working from a laptop at your kitchen table versus "the corner office." For the people who believe professional performance is tied to an office, I have to fake it. But sometimes this backfires.

My Assistant, the Six-year-old

I was negotiating an important contract for a client with one of the television networks. I was at home for the day as my oldest daughter was sick. My daughter was six years old at the time and during a break in negotiations, I literally ran to the bathroom for ten seconds. It was during those ten seconds that the network executives called back and my daughter answered the phone. She was chatting it up with the network people about how I was in the bathroom when I walked in. I wanted to die but, as it turned out, the key negotiator for this network was the mother of two boys.

My daughter's role as an "assistant" actually helped me establish some common ground and broke the ice a bit. As I got to know this woman more, she told me some of her stories about how she juggled family, work, and sanity. I find more than ever before people are willing to "admit" they are working from home or are on their cell phone driving their child somewhere. Until the day comes that having a family and being a mother is an acceptable part of business, I will continue to keep on faking it when I have to.

It Ain't Lyin' If You Are Working

Ironically, pretending to be at an office when I am nursing a sick kid at home hasn't caused my job performance to suffer. I negotiated one of the biggest contracts of my career on my beat-up kitchen table, using crayons to take notes. I did it out of necessity as I had a sick child and no backup that day.

Women are born multitaskers and this ability to juggle kicks in immediately when you become a mother. But I have to maintain the illusion that I am not on playground duty and that my kids don't exist with many people in the business world. This is slowly changing. Probably not fast enough but more businesses are starting to get it that moms can still do a great job even if they are not at the office nine to five.

Telecommuting, Flextime, Job-Share, and Part-Time Work

Judith Werner writes:

❖ *Years of surveys report 80 percent of mothers—working and at home alike—consistently say they wish they could work part time. The interesting question is, rather, why they're not getting it.*

❖ *Only 24 percent of working mothers now work part time. The reason so few do isn't complicated: most women can't afford to. Part-time work doesn't pay.*

Telecommuting, flextime, and job-sharing work schedules are options for balancing work and family. These concepts are not "mainstream" enough to be practical options for most women. I've been lucky to telecommute but it takes a certain mind-set from your client or employer. For example, our family dogs will bark ferociously at our eighty-year-old neighbor walking her poodle. Having three dogs loudly barking during a conference call can be distracting. Telecommuting is an option companies will use more often but it's still pretty new.

MOTHERHOOD IS GREAT TRAINING FOR BUSINESS

I worked full time in an office for most of my career. I've done the stay-at-home mom thing and I'm now working full time from home. I have friends that are scary-smart and skilled who believe they could not perform in a business or office setting because they lack experience. Ha!

Being around children all day is just like being in the business world, except that the children are usually more reasonable. I often tell my friends who have spent the last few years at home that they would be great in business because there are a lot of similarities between children and clients.

CHILDREN	CLIENTS
Throw Tantrums	Throw Tantrums
Act Unreasonable	Act Unreasonable
Are Self-Centered	Are Self-Centered

Children: You give them clear choices. "Pick the blue jacket or the brown jacket."

Clients: You give them clear choices. "You can have one new TV commercial or two radio commercials."

In both cases, you give the children/clients two choices. They feel like they are in charge when you really have control over the situation. I have told the first-grade teachers at my younger daughter's school that if they ever want to retire from teaching, they should go directly into the ad agency business. Their experience with six-year-olds is perfect for the advertising business.

If you are a Stay-at-Home Mom and you are worried that you don't have what it takes to work in the business world, don't sweat it! Staying home with kids is great preparation for working in an office. Additional perks of working in an office versus staying home with children: Your workday ends at a set time and you get to use the bathroom by yourself.

EVERY MOTHER IS A WORKING MOTHER, SO LET'S STICK TOGETHER

The battle between the Stay-at-Home and the Working Mothers is stupid. I have done full-time work and I have had times when I was not employed by anyone. I will not say that I "didn't work," because whoever says staying at home full time with children is not working has never done it.

Moms who work in offices, moms who work part time, moms who work from home, and moms who stay home to take care of the kids all have a lot in common and shouldn't waste time battling one another. The reality is that moms, especially White Trash Moms, can unite and support one another.

All of us need to work together to crush the unreachable standards of perfection that exist for modern moms. It just takes one White Trash Mom at a time.

If you are having a rough time of things and you're getting down on yourself, just remember that most of the other mothers out there are doing the same thing. We are breaking new ground so we have to make it up as we go along.

Sometimes you fail. Sometimes you win.

And it's always five o'clock somewhere.

The Zen of the
White Trash Mom

If you are living off the grid you don't have to worry about inter-acting with school, other moms, and families. Since most of us live in the real world, we need to keep two principles in mind at all times:

1. Blend in and be a part of the community enough to benefit your child.
2. Do not become too caught up in political games, as your actions impact your child.

It is being a White Trash Mom that enables you to walk the line between these two principles. Grab whatever you're drink-ing and follow along.

Going from Triple A to the Major Leagues

Getting your children into "real" school is not for the faint of heart.

It used to be that moms dropped off their kids at school and that was it. In these days of parenting as a competitive sport, we need to bring a little more to the game. Keep it in perspective but you also need to think of working the school system as you would taking on a new part of your job. Look at it as another requirement for your degree as a "mom."

If You Are Promoted at Your Job,
You Usually Ask Some Basic Questions

1. What is appropriate to wear?
2. When does everyone go to lunch?
3. Can I put my Pee-wee Herman doll on my desk?

If You Enrolled in a Course for Additional Certification for
Your Degree, You Would Ask Some Basic Questions

1. What materials do I need?
2. Is there anyone who has taken this course before? Can I get the notes?
3. What's the scoop on the teacher? Does he like to give pop quizzes or does he like it when people ask questions?
4. Can I sleep in class if I sit in the back row?

Please note that question number 3 from the work scenario and question number 4 from the school scenario might not apply to everyone. I was simply taking examples from my own office and school experiences.

Putting your kids into school requires that you find out some of the basic information that you would ask for a new class or new job.

DEALING WITH OTHER PARENTS

You need to be able to play nice and work nice with the other parents.

You may have nothing in common with them but you are thrown together because of your kids. Make it work.

Here are some tips from White Trash Mom on how you can play well with others.

Serious Business of Childhood

The White Trash Mom philosophy is very much about taking your role as a parent at the school seriously but it's also about keeping a sense of humor. Just like at work, you have to be careful and smart in your interactions. Arm yourself with information, work with the other parents, but have a cold beer waiting for you at home.

Queen Bee Moms and Kingpin Dads

Rosalind Wiseman wrote a book about dealing with other parents at school. It's called *Queen Bee Moms and Kingpin Dads* and it's an awesome resource for dealing with other parents at your children's school. She writes:

It's important to establish boundaries with other parents even in situations that don't affect you directly. You've probably gone to a parent meeting where someone hijacked the floor regarding a particular issue, dumping all over people who held contrary views.

You likely decided not to say or do anything: You didn't have strong feelings on that issue so you said to yourself that you should let the people who care duke it out.

Yours was part of the collective response: "Oh, her again. Just hear her out; she always does this."

Although you might have the luxury of leaving PTA meetings and heaving a sign of relief that you didn't have to deal with obnoxious parents, there's someone else who will: your child.

He or she will have to deal with those parents in a host of ways—from accepting their curriculum changes to putting up with their children. And since kids often behave in ways similar to their parents, should you really sigh with relief that you don't have to deal with these people when your child goes to a school where their children feel they have the run of the place?

Being a part of your child's school and volunteering in some way is a very basic and necessary part of your job as a parent. I have some tips for how to stay out of the politics in your community but you need to be involved in some manner because the school needs you.

NO EXCUSES

You might say that you can't help at your kid's school because you work full time. Or you have three little ones at home and so you can't go to the classroom or do lunchroom duty. It's time to stop the excuses and figure out how you can contribute. It's okay if you can't do some of these tasks. The point is to help in whatever way you can. Even if you can only help a little bit or your help is in nontraditional ways, pitching in *always helps your child*. That is the truth and you need to embrace it.

How to Volunteer

- Offer to create an e-mail list to notify parents about school events.
- Offer to help cut out some of the stuff the teacher needs for class. Some of the poor teachers develop carpal tunnel syndrome after they make four thousand red construction-paper squares.
- Offer to make reminder calls about the field trips to other parents.
- Buy the teacher a ten-dollar gift card from Target for school supplies.
- Offer to do things you can do at home or at work. There are many little things you can do. Just ask someone and she'll tell you.

❖ Bring extra Kleenex and Clorox Wipes to the class from time to time. Give extras, so the teacher doesn't have to buy them out of his or her pocket.

Now, while it is important to help, it's just as important to do what you can do without getting in over your head. That's where a little creative presentation goes a long way.

Creatives Don't Get Asked to Be PTA President

If you would rather stay on the edges of the community, to stay farther away from the political fray, then try the White Trash Mom "Artistic" Approach.

It's hard to say "no" when you get put on the spot and someone asks you to help with the latest fund-raiser or committee. My solution is to present an image to the community that says "I'm artistic" so that you are crossed off the short lists for some of the more political type of jobs. If they don't ask, you don't have to say "no."

Artistic types do not get *asked* to chair important committees. People respect and enjoy artistic types—they just don't want them running the budgets or speaking at meetings.

Being creative is one way you are *instantly* set apart in the school's pecking order. Creative types are asked to do the school newspaper. Or make a flyer or a poster for the bake sale. You can contribute but won't get left running the show.

DRESS FOR SUCCESS

Artistic Props—Get a pair of "geek" glasses if you don't have some already. Wear the glasses to school at pickup time.

Creative Clothing—Wear "artsy" clothes like hand-painted or tie-dye shirts, or T-shirts with "artsy" messages. Nothing too radical but something that says "I'm artistic."

Cowboy Boots—A good pair of cowboy boots can get you out of a whole bunch of meetings. Cowboy boots are funky and fun.

Other Good Props—Other props include frayed jeans, jean jackets, vintage coats—all of the things I am describing have a *flair* for the artistic and dramatic. You don't have to BE *artistic*—just look the part.

A White Trash Mom Case Study

One of my friends is a wonderful mom with several kids. This friend was constantly being asked to volunteer/chair/work on school projects. She did not seek out additional volunteer duties but was constantly barraged with calls to do more than her share of volunteer gigs at school. Why? She looks very capable. She has a bright smile, she dresses neatly, and she is friendly. In short, she appears to be very *responsible*. She is as WT as me but she is asked to participate in ten times as many volunteer things because she seems like she looks capable of doing the work.

I shared with my friend the secret of the White Trash Mom Artistic Props. She put a blond streak in her dark hair and purchased a pair of cowboy boots. Almost immediately, the *volunteer calls for her help were reduced by 25 percent*.

The next school year she frequently wore tie-dye shirts, which helped even more. She is still great and people still love her *and she has not hurt her children by doing this* but now she doesn't have to say no to the nice people who want her help. My friend just doesn't look as *responsible*. She looks more *artistic*. And she is a card-carrying member of the White Trash Mom nation.

TIPS FOR WHITE TRASH MOMS WHO WANT TO RUN THE SHOW

White Trash Moms can be great as school and community leaders. A part of the WTM mantra is to fight against the myth of perfection—if you are a leader you can make change from the inside and put some of these principles into action. You need to be sure that before you step up to the leadership plate you have the proper perspective and that your sense of humor is in full working order.

School leadership is often the territory of the *Muffia* (see chapter 6). You need to be sure that you can keep your cool and maintain a positive outlook so you can do the most good for the school and for your child. If you get into a power play or war of words with one of the queen bees, what's the point?

Some thoughts for you WTM leaders . . .

Listen More than You Talk

People listen to people who don't talk all the time. If you are a WTM in a leadership role, listen a whole bunch and speak very little at first.

Respect the Ways of the Past

You may have invented sliced bread but if you are in charge of the spring bake sale with Susie Homemaker . . . you're nothing but a rookie. Be respectful of how things have worked in the past so you can learn.

Change Is Slow, Be Patient

Change is slow so have patience with the people you are working with. Keep in mind that you can do more over the long haul if you can work with the other parents . . . even the Muffia. Stay the course and keep the long-term goal of fairness and equity in mind.

DEALING WITH TEACHERS AND SCHOOL ADMINSTRATORS

(Brown-nosing Teachers and Other School Survival Tactics)

Brown-nosing 101

Like it our not, part of your job as a parent is to help your child navigate the waters of his or her school. The hidden curriculum of the school is just as important as your child's schoolwork.

One aspect of helping your children at school is putting in extra effort with the teachers and school administration. In short, being a brown-noser helps. Before you shut this book in disgust, keep reading. You might not like the information but I am telling you from experience that it is a smart strategy and a way to help facilitate good will for your child with the people in charge.

Don't take White Trash Mom's word for this. Check out what some actual experts have to say about the political side of being a child.

Educator and child expert Richard Lavoie says:

> A child's social success will be largely determined by his abil-
> ity to influence those who are influential in his life. His rela-
> tionships with teachers, coaches, adult relatives, and other

significant grown-ups will dictate the depth and quality of his social life.

There are many political parts of childhood. You can help your child get along with teachers and authority figures by teaching them to be cooperative, responsive, and respectful. But your efforts to "grease the wheel" help your child's efforts.

I'm not suggesting you become a world-class brown-noser like me, but you'll be amazed how much sucking up can help your child. I am a natural "suck-up" to authority figures, as I have had a lifetime of practice at school and in my career. You don't have to be a total cheese ball but going out of your way to do more for the teachers and the school is good for your kid.

Reasons Why Brown-nosing Is Good

REASON #1—Teachers don't get enough positive reinforcement.
Being a teacher is a hard and thankless job. For the hours that are spent at the job, it is a low-paying career. Parents should help because it's the right thing to do and not enough people do it. If you can't volunteer for jobs during school hours, offer to make copies of homework sheets, ask what supplies are needed for the classroom, or buy a book for the library.

REASON # 2—Teachers are people.
I'm not suggesting your brown-nosing will change little Johnny's F to an A. But it is a fact that the teacher will give your little precious some slack and the benefit of the doubt if he or she likes your child.

REASON # 3—Build equity for a rainy day.
Sooner or later, your child or one of your children will do something very bad or will screw up in a major way in their school career. At some point in the time from ages five to eighteen there will be a crisis. It could be small, like your son wrote nasty words on the girls' bathroom wall. It could be a big crisis, like your daughter cheated on a major test or someone found some kids smoking pot at school. I don't know what the crisis will be, but it's a sure thing that there will be one.

Doing more for the teachers and school over the years will build your family and your children a little equity. It gets your family some "credit" in the school system. When the crisis comes up (and it will), you will "cash in your chips," cash in your sweat equity of good will that you've put in over the years to lessen the impact of the crisis.

These reasons for helping out the school and teachers may be brutal and calculating but they're facts of life. If you want to read something nice, go read a fairy tale. This is reality and sometimes it isn't pretty.

Blue Print for Brown-nosing

Every school is different. What works in Seattle, Washington, might be insulting in Tyler, Texas. You need to do your homework and ask your White Trash Mom mentors to find out more about your specific school.

However, there are a few things that are common in nearly

every school that you need to be aware of in order to be the best "Eddie Haskell" you can be.

THE SCHOOL SECRETARY AS QUEEN

In nearly every school, there is a school secretary or administrative assistant. A woman usually holds these positions. In most schools, this woman is *really* in charge.

Principals come and go. Vice principals and headmasters go to lunches and meetings. The school secretary is in charge of the daily functioning and decisions in the school. Usually but not always this person has the following traits:

❖ She has been at the school for a hundred years.
❖ She knows everyone and everything about everyone at the school.
❖ She is powerful.
❖ She is feared by most or all of the parents.

The school secretary or administrative assistant can usually make your life easy or make it a living hell. Right after enrolling your child at the school, find out who has this position in the school office. After you find out, if you are following the rules that White Trash Mom has given you, you will immediately start sucking up to this person and "kissing the ring" of power. Suggestions for ways to endear yourself to the most powerful person at the school:

Bring Her Coffee

Coffee is the lifeblood of any teacher or school secretary. If your job revolves around children, coffee is vital. Bring her coffee and she'll love you.

Volunteer for Clerical Duties

It will often fall to the school office staff to coordinate the massive amounts of paperwork involved with weekly school newsletters or school bulletins. Offer to make copies for them at Kinko's. Ask to help deliver items to the classroom if needed.

Remember the Holidays

Most people *do not* think of the school office staff when the holidays roll around. I pay special attention to the school secretary (and other staff) at the holidays. I try to purchase gifts that are practical and thoughtful.

The Bottom Line on Brown-nosing

Don't let it all hang out. The lesson for this chapter is that your interaction at school, in sports, and with other parents is not about you. It's about your child. Your child is at the same "job" for six to eight years in elementary school. Your actions have a huge impact on your child's experience at school. Don't screw it up.

You might whine:
I want to *express* myself!
I want to *be who I am*!
I'm not a "soccer mom!

But it's not about you! Quit your whining and grow up.
    Nobody ever said being a mother was easy.

5

ABC

School Talk

Teachers and other parents communicate to you about your child, in many ways. When you are new to the world of elementary school politics, you actually believe that what the teachers are saying is what they mean.

But after you have been in the trenches you start to catch on. What the teachers say and what they mean are as different as day and night. For all kinds of reasons, the teachers must communicate in code. Let me show you what I mean.

Communication is a two-way street. Every school is different, but for the most part, please trust White Trash Mom when I tell you some of the cardinal sins of communicating with teachers. Nothing will get you on a teacher's blacklist faster than committing one of these.

WHAT THEY SAY	WHAT THEY MEAN
Max is very creative and energetic.	Max is from hell. He needs to be medicated.
I hope I'm not catching you at a bad time . . .	Call 911. The sh** is going to hit the fan.
Scott needs to apply himself more to his studies.	Scott is going to be your worst teenage nightmare. Look for military schools ASAP.
Mrs. Lamar, I left you a voice mail about your daughter . . .	Since I have had to call you more than one time, it is clear to me that you are a very bad mother. I have already told the other teachers.
Wanted to remind you about the Food Drive . . .	You are an airhead. It's a wonder you haven't lost your children yet.
A gentle reminder about the money for the field trip.	Let me draw you a picture. I need the $3.00 or your kid sits in the lunchroom all day. Do I look like a bank?
Terri is a bubbly girl with lots and lots of friends.	Terri will be the class tramp. I'll be amazed if she's not living in a conversion van with her boyfriend Steve by age sixteen.
Do you have time after school for a quick meeting?	Bring your attorney. One of the kids set off stink bombs in the bathroom again.
Tessa tells me her favorite show is *Trashy Reality TV II*.	You are a terrible mother. You'll be lucky if I don't hotline you.
Shawn has been eating glue again . . .	Your son is a complete deviant. If I were you, I would just start over. He's a lost cause.

COMMUNICATION 101 WITH TEACHERS

Do Not Tell the Teacher You Are Too Busy and You'll Call Back

This seems obvious but I have to say it. If a teacher who has a class of twenty students is taking the time to call you, the parent of one of his or her students, you need to pay close attention. Nothing is more important. If the house is on fire, tell the teacher to hold the phone for a minute and have the neighbor call 911. It's big if the teacher calls you so don't screw it up.

Do Not Make a Teacher Leave You More Than One Message or E-mail

Same rule applies. If the teacher is contacting you, *do not* make him or her have to do it again. No excuses on this one.

Don't Tell the Teacher that He or She "Must Be Mistaken"

Even if your kid didn't set off the bomb in the school bathroom, *do not* make the mistake of immediately defending your kid. You can and should defend your child but if you immediately start telling the teacher that what that individual is telling you is wrong, you are on your way to the blacklist. Listen. Listen. Listen. Act or defend later. Thank them for letting you know.

Don't Let the Teacher Down on a Promise

If you say you'll bring napkins for the party or you'll help them with the bulletin board, make sure you do it. Teachers are stretched way thin and they'll remember it if you blow them off. Offering to help and then not doing it is worse than doing nothing.

Why Does It Matter So Much How I Act to the Teachers?

If you have to ask this question, please come over to my house so I can slap you. After a slap, let me explain. First, you should be helpful to the teachers because they have a hard job and because they are with your child for a great deal of time every day. Second, you are an idiot if you think that your actions with one teacher don't impact your child for the balance of the time your child attends that school!

Teachers work with other teachers. They talk about work. Work involves your children. If you are a jerk and you make one of the teachers mad, you can bet your life that by the end of the following school day, every teacher in the building has got the scoop. It's a scientific fact that gossip spreads faster in the teacher's lounge than in any other room in the school.

Bare-Butt Analogy

For those of you who are *really* dense, let me put this in graphic terms. Let's say you were at a holiday office party and you got drunk and made photocopies of your bare butt. After you made fifty copies of your bare butt, you decide to display these pictures for the entire office to see. In addition, you send a group e-mail to everyone in the office telling him or her where to see the photocopies of your bare butt.

Pulling a stunt like that would wreck your career at most offices. (Except at an ad agency. It would probably get you promoted at an ad agency.) Acting mean or snotty or rude to a teacher is the mom equivalent of making a photocopy of your bare butt. It's a screaming signal that you are an idiot and it puts a giant black mark by your name in the roll books for all of the teachers at the school. This is bad, by the way. Once again, my message to you is to be on your best behavior with all teachers and administrators. What you do today will follow your child forever.

COMMUNICATION 101 WITH OTHER PARENTS

Think of it this way: The other parents are the people you work with in your job as a parent. Approach interaction with them with the same amount of care as you do your office coworkers. Find a way to get along and work with them because it benefits your kids in the long run.

If you are new to the world of "parent-to-parent" communication, let me give you some examples. Check with the White Trash Moms in your community to get the local flavor but on the opposite page are some "red flags" of parent-to-parent communication you should be aware of.

We will get into some of the more complicated communication issues in chapter 6 on "The Muffia." You don't have to be the homecoming queen of parental units but make every effort to be fair, thoughtful, and kind in your communication and interaction

WHAT PARENTS SAY	WHAT PARENTS MEAN
We are starting a new baseball team since so many kids signed up.	Your son sucks at baseball, so he should join the team with the "B" players.
My daughter, Janie, said there was a problem at soccer practice today.	Your daughter was picking on my kid at soccer today; what are you going to do about it?
Do you think you can work at the fourth-grade booth at school carnival?	Get off your lazy butt and help us, for God's sake.

with the other parents. That being said, there are parents who can send you running, screaming, for the hills.

These parents are those you should avoid or approach with extreme caution:

The Controller

She monitors everything her child eats, says, and does. She constantly refers to her child and her child's activities in the *plural*. "We were in Girl Scouts" or "We did not make the swim team." She keeps a tight leash on her child that will result in complete rebellion at a later age. There is jail time or an unwed pregnancy in her offspring's future.

The Best-Friend Parent

If you hear the words, "my child is my best friend" . . . *run!* Do not pass go. Do not collect two hundred dollars. Do not let your kid spend a lot of time over at the "best-friend" household. These parents don't want to parent, they want to be kids. I want to be friends with my daughters. . . . when they are adults. The "BF" parents usually have kids who marry young to a forty-five-year-old college professor because they are seeking a parental figure.

The Perfect Mom

If someone spends a lot of time telling you about how she is a perfect mom or that her family is perfect . . . *look for bodies buried in the basement. Seriously.* It is ALWAYS the "perfect" families and moms that have the really ugly and dangerous secrets that come out years later.

BULLIES

A recent study revealed that one out of every three middle-school-age kids was bullied in some way. In that particular study, one third of the kids were bullied every day. You need to be aware of bullying as it happens everywhere and the chances are high that your kid will be a target. It's sad but it's very true.

Some useful tactics in helping your child become more resilient to bullies:

- ❖ Make sure your child has a variety of activities, interests, and friends.
- ❖ Try to get your child involved in a nonschool activity or to have regular interaction with friends who don't go to the same school.

❖ This is good for all kids of all ages but this is especially helpful when the horrid middle-school years are upon your family.

❖ When the girls or boys are mean and your child is left out, it's a bonus to be able to have some buddies from the swim team to do things with.

❖ Kids with Learning Disabilities or ADD are often targets for bullies, so read up on the issue. The more you know about your child's learning issue the better you can help with teachers, other parents, and bullies.

Talking to Parents of Bullies

Here is the one bit of advice I will give you about dealing with the parents of a bully. Are you ready?

Never, ever talk to the parents of a bully about the problem.

I know you're thinking I'm wrong. How hard can it be, after all? If there is a problem between children, you think you can simply discuss the issues calmly with the parents of the bully because, after all, we're all adults, right? Here is what I have to say to you if you are having these calm and logical thoughts:

ARE YOU COMPLETELY INSANE?

Talking to parents of bullies is bad for your child. If it has gotten so bad that you need to talk to the parents of the bully, then it's too late. You cannot talk to them and get any results. In fact, if you talk to the parents of a kid who is bullying your kid, it will make things far worse! This is a law of parenting and you must trust me that I know about this from experience. It will not work and it does not work. Let me tell you why. Some bullies come from perfectly normal and nice families. The kids are the "bad seed" in a family that is caring and loving. However, the "bad seed" type of bully is not the norm. For the most part, kids who are jerks have parents who are jerks. As the old saying goes, "The apple doesn't fall far from the tree," so it's rather insane of you to think that a bully has parents who would be reasonable. It should be no surprise that some of the snobby moms have children who turn out to be bullies. If the parents have a sense of entitlement, the children act the same way.

PAVING THE ROAD FOR YOUR CHILD

Your communication efforts with the adults at the school and other parents affect your child in dramatic ways. Do your homework and tread carefully. Think of yourself last and put your child first.

6

The Muffia

Now it's time to take on the scourge of every schoolyard—the Muffia. It is important to me that you completely understand what the Muffia is, what it stands for, and why it goes against everything we, as White Trash Moms, stand for.

It should be noted that I did not coin the term "Muffia." No, that credit, my WT friends, goes to the talented Allison Pearson and her esteemed book *I Don't Know How She Does It*.

It's on the required reading list for all White Trash Moms. A great book is made into a classic by some of the lingo Pearson created.

My own definition of the Muffia, for those of you who missed it the first time, is as follows:

Mean and snobby mothers who usually run the school your child attends. Being a part of the Muffia is being mean and not being real. It's about keeping up a totally bogus and stupid

standard of perfection that is unrealistic. It is taking mother-
hood and making it a spectator sport.

In every school, in every city across these great United
States, there is an unwritten code of conduct for motherhood
performance. While different in each school and town, it is a
fact that in every school community there is a small group of
mothers that we call the Muffia.

The "uniform" of the Muffia may vary according to your geo-
graphic area, but make no mistake, the group exists in every
school, and its presence can't be ignored.

The Muffia is the enemy. They are the enemy because they
embody and uphold the myth of perfection. They are the enemy
because they look down their noses at moms who don't meet
their standards of perfection.

To be a part of the evil Muffia means that you feel you are
entitled. You are better than other mothers, and you have the
right to act in a way that properly represents your station in the
community.

What's the problem, you might ask? Nuke them! Destroy
them. Ignore these beasts of motherly hell. As if it were that
simple.

FIGHT THE MUFFIA AND YOUR KIDS LOSE

If you ignore the unwritten Muffia rules or rebel against the system, your children—not you—will pay the price. So, you have
to be very careful in how you "fight" the enemy. You have to
stand up for some things but other times you just have to play
along. You need to, as they say, choose your battles.

You don't have to like it.

And that doesn't mean you can't have a little fun while you are playing along.

To start with, here are few warning signs you could be battling when you are dealing with a member of the evil Muffia.

Spawn with Names that Sound Like Street Names

"One" hates to generalize, but with spawn whose names are Bluffington, Harper, Waverly, and Linden, how can "one" help it? And who can tell the difference between the boys' names and the girls' names? Really. Can you? (The first two were girls, and the second two were boys . . . apparently.)

Chatting with Friends in the Pickup Line as a Hundred Cars Wait

Another red flag for possible Muffia activity is "chatting while everyone else waits." A common sign of a card-carrying member of Muffia Central is when the mom disregards the rules and ignores the hundred-car waiting line at school while she has a very animated "chat" with one of her friends.

Everyone is guilty of being clueless sometimes. But if you notice that it's the same woman holding up the line at school pickup, you can pretty much count on the fact she's one of them.

How Many Introductions?

If you've been introduced to another mom more than three times and each time this person acts like she has never laid eyes on you, you're probably dealing with a member of the Muffia. I am the worst person with names but if I can't remember a name of another parent, I am still courteous. It's the entitlement thing again—she's too cool to bother with people outside her radar.

Looks Can Be Deceiving

If a mom dresses like a million bucks or plays tennis a ton, is she a Muffy? Absolutely, positively no! Don't judge by appearances—the whole point of being a WTM is to give more people a chance and to be fair. Don't judge if you don't want to be judged.

Now, the mere fact that these women "look" good does not automatically place them in the category of Muffia. No, it's more about disdaining everyone else for his or her lack of perfection.

Additional Warning Signs for a Muffia Member

The Muffia, like other cold-blooded creatures, must stay warm. Usually the Muffia wear furs or expensive coats to keep warm and to show the community their wealth. The Muffia are usually but not *always* attractive and these she-devils usually have a low percentage of body fat.

   Hair—Styled and highlighted in a "natural" way that is found only in the most expensive salons.
   Facial Features—Her eyes can produce sparks at a moment's notice. She has a big smile but like a crocodile, she can eat you for lunch.

Clothes—She wears chic clothes, even if she's just finished working out at the gym. Costume jewelry does not touch her skin. Her nails are freshly manicured and prepared to claw your eyes out if you cross her. Her feet have the latest designer shoes so that she can walk over everyone.

If you see a woman matching the description above, walk away quickly. Do not attempt to engage her on your own unless you are an experienced White Trash Mom.

Let's be careful out there, ladies. and remember that war is hell.

The Muffia Is Our Enemy But We Have a Spy

In the war against all that is bad in motherhood, you'll be happy to know we have in our midst a mole. A spy. A recovering member of the Muffia. Tacky Princess, my comrade and partner in blogging, is, in fact, a former member of the Muffia.

Her cover will be blown once the book is published but the information from the "inside" has been invaluable. She is risking a great deal in her fight for truth and justice. She will probably have to leave her hair colorist once the word gets out that she talked. She has already turned in her gym membership. But this brave mom is speaking out because she knows what's right. Here are a few nuggets of wisdom from Tacky Princess:

Don't Judge by Appearance Alone

Muffys come in all shapes and sizes. They live in every zip code, and they can even be like sheep in wolves' clothing. Just because a woman wears capris, bejeweled flip-flops, and a headband does not mean that she's a Muffy. You have to look beyond the uniform. Likewise, you may be speaking to someone who appears to be normal—on the outside. They may not be dressed in the perfect tennis set, complete with the perfect manicure and the perfectly bleached and veneered teeth. But their razor-sharp conversation skills are what will give this type of Muffy away. Allow me to illustrate. Recently, I had this conversation with a new acquaintance who, unbeknownst to me, was most definitely a Muffy under the guise of a normal woman. Perhaps her transformation wasn't complete. Perhaps I had just caught her on several "bad manicure/my clothes are at the cleaners/haven't had time to get my hair colored" sorts of days. I don't know.

Here is a chilling rundown of a recent Muffia encounter I had in the school parking lot. The woman in question did not seem like the typical Muffy to an untrained eye. Read and learn, ladies.

Trashy Princess: *Hi, Jane.*
Jane: *Oh, hi! Can you believe it's already three-fifteen? And Friday? This week has gotten—lost!*
TP: *Yeah, I know what you mean . . . I haven't gotten nearly as much done this week as I intended.*
Jane: *Oh, me neither. My car [pointing at a perfectly shined late model SUV] was in the shop, so I had to use the old Mercedes all week. [Okay, so they have the new SUV, the old Mercedes, plus the husband's car, whatever that is . . . just trying to keep up here.] It was*

a major hassle. And then, Hayleigh's volleyball club had four practices this week instead of three, and she still had her two regular dance classes and three soccer practices. So, I had to cancel my bleaching, my mani/pedi, and don't even get me started on the dog. He hasn't been groomed in three weeks. I can't take him anywhere. It's just too embarrassing. He's even got a hot spot right above his eye.

TP: [stammering] Wow, have . . . have . . . have you lost weight?

Jane: What? No, I haven't made it to the gym since Wednesday, and that was only for an hour before my tennis lesson. Do you take lessons?

TP: Oh no. I just sort of bat it around now and then.

Jane: Are you kidding? You have to take lessons. It's the only way to improve your game. I won't play unless I've had at least two lessons per week. Otherwise, I just embarrass myself. Same with the kids. I told them they cannot play unless they have at least two lessons a week. It's the only way. Bill thinks I'm crazy, but there it is.

TP: Uhmm . . .

Jane: [looking past me, scanning the parking lot for other moms . . .] Tiffany! Over here [waits as Tiff approaches, in all of her Muffia splendor]!! Did you see what Marie was wearing at the social yesterday? Those capris [pointing down and smiling appreciatively]? Hey, cute sandals, by the way . . . Anyway, has she gained weight or what? And where was her husband? I heard they're splitsville . . . and she missed coffee again this morning, so . . .

TP: [slipping away unnoticed . . . approaching another WTM] Just kill-me-now!

Tips for "Fighting" the Muffia

All WT Moms should be grateful for the top-secret information we've been able to download from our spy, Tacky Princess.

Going up against the Muffia is a tricky business, to say the least. Believe me, I speak from experience. Whether your children get along beautifully in school or they struggle, the Muffia can present a *huge* problem for the White Trash Mom.

First, you have to understand what the Muffia are really saying to you. Here is a quick guide to interpreting the Muffia Code:

WHAT THEY SAY	WHAT THEY MEAN
Is the picture from the class collage done for the school auction yet?	We spent forty-five minutes at the coffee shop this morning discussing your lack of follow-through with the auction project. What is it going to take for you to get your act together?
How sweet.	You are an idiot.
Is Laura still taking violin?	Is your child still a total geek? I'm so glad I pulled my precious from that awful music thing.
Where are you going for spring break?	Do you have the cash to give your kids a real vacation this year?
How cute! Where did you get those shoes?	I would d-i-e before I wore those shoes. Doesn't anyone care what they look like? My God!

WHAT THEY SAY	WHAT THEY MEAN
(*Whispering*). How is Scott?	I think your son is very different and this is very bad. I hope he can find work picking up trash on the side of the highway or whatever it is people who are different do. (*Shudder*)
Please call at least one other mom in your class to remind them about the school carnival.	Call one of the other moms in the class or you will know the meaning of pain and suffering.
It was nothing.	I spent three friggin' hours making the icing for the damn cake and I expect to get all the credit I deserve for it.
Thanks for asking about Kathy! She's super and loves state university. It's wonderful.	Kathy just told us she is a lesbian and she worships Satan. On the bright side, her grades are good.

Confronting Muffia Directly

Sometimes, no matter how hard you try you will find yourself going head-to-head with a member of the Muffia. It won't be pretty but by following my advice, you will survive.

Passive-Aggressive Engagement via Spook Patrol

Spook Patrol is a way that you can take action against those people who are evil. For those times when you can't fight back through conventional means, Spook Patrol is a way to mess with the beasts from the Muffia without direct confrontation; a way to mess with their small brains and make you feel just a little better.

You may call this ancient practice sick or twisted. But if you've never tried it, you really don't know what you're missing.

Spook Patrol is like Chinese water torture. It is not meant for short-term gain or reward. Like Chinese water torture, it is a drip-drip-drip system. Let me give you an example of Spook Patrol from my own life as a way of showing you how to use it.

Spook Patrol Case Study

When I was in college, I worked part time as a waitress in a steak house. The owner of this restaurant was the kindest, sweetest man to walk the face of the earth.

The manager of the restaurant was his demonic spawn-from-hell daughter, whom we will call Mary Beth. This woman hated my guts the first time she saw me.

MB pretty much hated all the college girls who worked at the restaurant but she had a special place in her cold heart for me. She made my life hell and I almost quit until one of my friends reminded me of the power of Spook Patrol. Beginning with my next shift at the steak house, I started using Spook Patrol.

❖ I volunteered to help the evil Mary Beth with hostess duties when the hostess called in sick.
❖ Another shift, I stayed late and helped with inventory.
❖ I made it a point to always ask at least three or four questions of the evil Mary Beth each time I worked.
❖ No matter what answer Mary Beth snarled at me I would always give her a huge smile.

I was always very professional and nice. I killed her with kindness.

After several shifts where I killed Mary Beth with kindness I began *the second phase of Spook Patrol*. With calculated precision, I started working into my conversations with the evil one a series of subtle put-downs designed to zing Mary Beth in a slow but effective manner. Dig, if you will, the following examples:

"Mary Beth, you look great in those pants. Have you lost weight?"

(The woman poured herself into her jeans every night so that everyone around her could enjoy her figure.)

"Mary Beth, is that red in your hair? I didn't know that they could highlight black hair with red highlights."

(She fancied herself a redhead. She looked like a circus clown on crack.)

After a few weeks of phase two Spook Patrol, Mary Beth treated me as a human. The point of putting Mary Beth on Spook Patrol was to show her that she didn't have power over me. She judged me the moment she saw me and I knew I would never change her. However, I used Spook Patrol to let Mary Beth know I didn't play her reindeer games. You mess with me, you mess with the whole trailerpark.

The Muffia Only Understand Power

The usual rules of interpersonal interaction don't apply if you are dealing with a true member of the Muffia. Like a terrorist, the Muffia understand only power. Unlike a terrorist, the Muffia use casseroles, cupcakes, and school plays as weapons. You can't fight "fair" or work out a compromise. You have to use the tools of communication the Muffia will understand.

Isn't Spook Patrol Immature and Petty?

Using Spook Patrol is quite immature and extremely petty. But when you must deal with the Muffia, harsh steps must be taken at times. Let me stress that there is a time and place to confront those who believe they are entitled to act like jerks.

Using Spook Patrol in some of your Muffia encounters makes sense in a twisted kind of way. You're not going to change an adult woman who views her children as accessories for social status. Trying to reason with a person who looks down on others for superficial reasons is a lost cause.

You can't constantly battle the Muffia on every issue because your child will pay the price. This is a fact. Using the ancient tactics of passive-aggressive behavior, Spook Patrol is a way to keep the Muffia a little afraid of you. Spook Patrol is also a way to show them (not tell them) that they shouldn't mess with you.

Never Use Spook Patrol in Anger

Spook Patrol, like the martial arts, should never be used to harm another mother. Never use Spook Patrol in an aggressive way. You only use SP to defend yourself if you are attacked. This is very important. Here are some very specific examples of Spook Patrol in action for you to study:

Example 1

Barfy Marcy bounces up to you at the soccer game. This is unusual as she pretends not to know you most of the time.

MARCY: Hi there! How did Molly do on that horrible test last week?

YOU: I'm not sure but I think she did okay. Math isn't her best subject.

MARCY: Parker got an A– but I was concerned about your cute Molly because I know she has a tutor for math.

YOU: Sure, thanks for asking but it's fine. Glad to know Parker is doing well. Hey . . . have you lost weight? You look great today. Your face isn't as puffy as it was when I saw you at Christmas.

MARCY: [Stunned, confused as she prides herself on her low-body-fat percentage] No, I'm still the same.

YOU: Well, whatever you're doing, keep it up. It really agrees with you [big smile and walk away].

Analysis of Barfy Marcy Encounter

You know that Marcy wouldn't walk across the street to pee on you if you were on fire. Based on this fact, you know the only reason she is coming over to speak to you is because she wants to make sure you know how superior Parker is compared to your daughter. Allow Barfy Marcy to brag, then give her a dose of Spook Patrol. Smile and walk away.

Example 2
You are setting up for the school carnival. A random sports Muffia mom that you don't know very well slithers up to talk to you.

> **RANDOM MOM:** I'm sorry to hear that Joe didn't make the football team this year.
> **YOU:** Yeah, it was tough for him but he'll just try harder next year.
> **RM:** Chandler made the team and is playing quarterback but he knows he has to really work hard this season.
> **YOU:** That's wonderful. You must be very proud of him. I hope you don't think this is a personal question but where do you get your hair done?
> **RM:** Huh?
> **YOU:** I was noticing your highlights and it's such an unusual color. I really like the brassy-meets-blond look. Would you mind giving me the name of your stylist or do you do it yourself?
> **RM:** [Confused, as she pays two hundred dollars per session for a highlights and prides herself on her blond hair looking natural] Huh?

Additional Muffia Smart Bombs

❖ Great sweater, by the way. I have a potholder/blanket
  at home that has the same pattern.

❖ I *love* the shoes! Didn't I see those at Target last week?
  I almost bought a pair.

❖ I saw your precious Lucy last weekend at a movie . . .
  she is very *popular* with the boys, isn't she?

❖ I love the way you've been highlighting your hair. The
  yellow highlights are so bright. . . . I like the way your
  stylist blended some red into them, it's so *bold*.

❖ You're going to————during spring break? Isn't that
  the island that had the————epidemic? I'm sure your
  hotel won't be near the infected areas. . . .

❖ Muffy! I *heard* that you lost weight! My goodness, they
  were *right*. You *look* fabulous.

Last Word on the Muffia

The Muffia has far less to do with the external things like how
you look, how you cook, what you wear, or how you fix your hair.
It has to do with the inside stuff like being mean to other mothers (and sometimes even their children). Being a Muffy is about
being hurtful and superficial. It's about upholding a totally bogus
and stupid standard of perfection that is completely unrealistic
and, ultimately, damaging to the whole family. It is about *not
supporting* your fellow mothers but tearing them down. It's about
snobbery and condescension and it's wrong.

Let's be careful out there.

7

School Volunteerism and Your "ROI"

Every school needs parents to help with the field trips, getting supplies for the classrooms, the bake sale, the auction, and the other functions. I don't recommend blowing off all opportunities for volunteering as it will be noticed and not favorably. Also, if you don't give to the school, it is your child who suffers, not you. Your actions impact the way your child is viewed in the school community. If you don't help out, the people in the community resent your lack of help. But they won't tell you . . . they'll just take it out on your child. Everything you do reflects on your child. You don't have to go into the school every day or commit to a huge amount of time to get your volunteer hours in. As a White Trash Mom, you will learn to volunteer in a way that meets your criteria and doesn't suck the life and time out of you.

MAXIMUM BROWNIE POINTS FOR LEAST
AMOUNT OF WORK POSSIBLE

The bottom line of the White Trash Mom school volunteering is that you need to be able to get the maximum proverbial bang for your volunteering buck. Some jobs have greater return for the investment of time. A good White Trash Mom helps at school in the areas or subjects that provide the utmost number of brownie points for the least amount of work possible. My pal Tacky Princess and I like to use the "Volunteer ROI Analysis" test when considering school volunteer duties.

Volunteer ROI Analysis, or Return on Investment

This scientific-sounding term simply refers to the perceived benefit one receives in relation to the countless hours one spends as a volunteer slave. Benefits may include items such as spending more time with your children and observing how your child fits into the overall social scene at school. Keep in mind that what your little cherubs *say* is going on and what is *actually* transpiring is not always the same. Volunteering is like being a mole in their world. Likewise, the opportunity to spy on the school administration is always a bonus.

Always figure out the ROI before any volunteer situation. Time spent reading this section of the book will save you hours of agony down the line.

As a former card-carrying member of the Muffia and a recovering compulsive volunteer, Tacky Princess is an expert in Volunteer ROI Analysis. Read her words of wisdom, campers.

This woman has logged more volunteer hours than anyone I know.

Tacky Princess VOLUNTEER ROI ANALYSIS FOR BEGINNERS

All volunteering is not created equal. Your investment of time and effort is far greater with some "jobs" than with others. That is to say, certain volunteer gigs have a much better White Trash Mom Volunteer ROI Analysis than others.

The Sweet Spot: High Visibility/Low Volunteer Hours

The combination of high visibility/low volunteer hours is the White Trash Mom's goal in any volunteer situation.

Get Good Intelligence from Multiple Sources

Like the scouts, a good White Trash Mom is prepared.

Make sure you have the correct information from veteran mothers for the volunteer opportunities at hand. Don't trust the opinions of rookie mothers who haven't yet been in the trenches. Get the real scoop from at least three different mothers about which volunteer jobs are high visibility/low volunteer hours.

Being a room mom (class mom) could be a cakewalk in Portland, Oregon . . . but a hellish nightmare in Houston, Texas. You have to get confirmation from multiple sources so you can be sure it's reliable. What is easy for one mom might be a nightmare for you.

Wild-card Factors in Volunteer ROI Analysis

There are some wild-card factors in your volunteer decision:

Is there alcohol involved?

Any chore is better with a little Happy Hour!

Are there weekly meetings?

Certain volunteer jobs have good ROI Analysis but there is a great deal of weekly upkeep. Even if it's a good gig, if you can't be reliable with the weekly meetings, you need to pass.

Who are the usual suspects?

Any job can be fun if you are working with the right people.

Is there a great deal of paperwork?

Please note that volunteer jobs, which involve a high concentration of paperwork, could be a nightmare.

Are you able to work off-site or at home?

There are benefits to being able to perform your volunteer duties from home or from your office. One huge advantage of doing volunteer work at your office is that your boss is paying you for doing things you are supposed to be doing after work.

The Child Visibility Index

This is one of the most important segments of the ROI wild cards. One of the big reasons you donate time and become involved at school is so your kids will know that you are there and that you are interested. Even if they pretend they don't know you, they are secretly glad you're there.

Review of the Basics of Volunteer ROI Analysis

* ❖ Your goal is to hit the "sweet spot" of high visibility/ low volunteer hours.
* ❖ Get good intelligence from multiple sources
* ❖ Wild-card factors

I can't stress enough to you the importance of finding out the correct information from your moms in the field. Knowing that every situation and every school is different, I will attempt to give you a broad overview of most school volunteer situations.

ANALYSIS OF VOLUNTEER JOBS

Each job analysis includes an overview of the job along with notes from Tacky Princess. Following each is a brief ROI Analysis from White Trash Mom.

PLAYGROUND DUTY

Time Required: One hour
Frequency Required: Once or twice a month
Visibility: High

Tacky Princess COMMENTS

Okay, let me say straight out of the chute that this was not a good match for me. Never mind the fact that you have to endure freezing temperatures, cold winds, and your own children ignoring your very existence. Sap that I am, I was nearly in tears half the time I did playground duty, purely because of the angst I witnessed on little kids' faces on the playground. As a mother of two girls, I am only too well aware that girls can be one catty bunch of tigresses, but the things that I have observed over the years on our school playground would make the worst of "Conniving Clique Chicks" (CCC) from your childhood look like a choir practice.

Now, if those girls saw me watching them, their behavior changed miraculously. They might even run right up to me and exclaim, "Oh hi, how are you today?"

Worse were the ones who would see me watching (in horror . . . trying to decide as an "active" parent how to react . . .) and continue but only after turning their backs, so I could no longer actually "see" or "hear" what was transpiring. If the victim spoke up later, these bullies knew that it would be the victim's word against all of theirs. And with their persuasive tongues and sickly sweet, innocent-sounding voices, they would invariably come off appearing to be the victims themselves. Unbelievable.

Don't even get me started on what happens if you in your role as the "monitor" do act. Chances are the CCC's are children of women like Tiffany and Muffy. Trust me when I tell you that these moms are card-carrying members of the Muffia. And when you cross the Muffia, be on the lookout for a horse's head in your bed. So, unless you have nerves (and emotions) of steel, I'd cross playground duty off your list of potential volunteer activities.

 **White Trash Mom** ROI ANALYSIS

High Visibility/Low Volunteer Hours
No alcohol involved, no weekly meetings, no paperwork, and no need for off-site work. There are pros to this job but you might need therapy after a session of recess duty. Pro: Good if you can handle the brutality of the playground. Con: Not everyone has the stomach for it.

PAPER CUTTING

Time Required:	Two hours
Frequency Required:	Once a month
Visibility:	Low

Tacky Princess COMMENTS

Usually requested of moms with children who are in the lower grades, this job is easy but boring. However, you might get lucky and be assigned with another White Trash Mom for this duty. If, on the other hand, you get stuck with someone who is about as fun as watching paint dry, then it will be a long couple of hours. The job involves cutting out shapes or numbers for the teachers, who need paper items for their bulletin board or class projects. Teachers appreciate this job. Note to first-timers: Get the manicure after doing paper-cutting duty. Chances are you'll wind up with a few paper cuts and a hangnail or two. On the bright side, you'll be warm (or cool, depending on the season) for the duration of your volunteer stint, and there is very little likelihood of crossing paths with the Muffia, as they tend to prefer considerably higher-profile posts. Not my personal preference, but you are the ultimate judge on this one.

White Trash Mom ROI ANALYSIS

Low Visibility/Low Volunteer Hours

No alcohol involved, no weekly meetings, no paperwork.

It's a good gig if you can take the work home and cut while you are watching reality TV. Pro: This is also a great way to get brownie points with teachers if you can't volunteer in the classroom! Con: No points for child visibility but it's a good solid job. I did this when I was working full time and it helped the teachers.

LUNCHROOM PARENT

Time Required: Three hours
Frequency Required: One or two times per
                     month
Visibility: Medium to high

 Tacky Princess COMMENTS

Now, right off the bat, I have to correct the name. While most schools do the politically correct thing and call this post Lunchroom Parent, in all of my years of volunteering in the lunchroom, I have only seen four dads.

Let's face it. A dad is almost never a Lunchroom Parent. My hat is off to those dads who have done it. They seem to actually enjoy it (gasp!), and you know, I think their kids are genuinely happy to have them there.

When I was growing up in public school, I do not remember a single unpaid person working in our lunchroom. However, in the parochial schools where the children all dress like identical little plaid clones of one another, complete with matching headbands, scrunchies, and socks that come at least two inches above the tops of their shoes (can't show those sexy ankles!), there is no money left in the pot at the end of the day to pay people to run the lunchroom. So— once again, it falls to the parents. And let's just call a spade a spade here—the moms. Our school has three or four paid employees and a band of volunteers. My White Trash comrades, in my opinion this is the worst volunteer post that there is. Here's why.

As you may or may not know, one signs up for these little jobs at the beginning of the school year. So, they get your commitment up front, and you can only claim so many cramps, migraines, and hangovers before being discovered as the true slacker that you are.

Being a cafeteria lady was never one of my career aspirations, even as a small girl. Here, just a few of the reasons . . .

❖ *The HAIRNET—um-hmmm . . . hairnet. We have to wear them. My children look on gleefully as I dish out the pears while sporting this piece of 1950s history. Just call me June Cleaver.*

❖ *No samples—not even one little crumb! In the old days, we could scarf down the deformed brownies in between shifts of students but no longer. Not since we became part of the government-subsidized food program. They literally make us count the packages of crackers that we set out, and we can't even have one of those.*

❖ *We are made to ration out the food as if we may run out at any moment. You would think we were living in the Depression. Like it would break the budget to give little Bruiser that extra green bean on his tray.*

❖ *We have to go around and collect the reusable plastic spoons and forks as the kids finish eating (so they don't accidentally throw them away). If they do so, we have to make the kids either rifle through the trash for the seven-cent spoon (and how disgusting is that?), or we have to do it ourselves (as if . . .).*

❖ Cleaning the tables—Have you ever cleaned up after
  seventy-five first graders ate chicken-fried steak, mashed
  potatoes, gravy, and canned fruit? Not pretty. And don't
  even get me started on taco day . . .

When I got my bachelor's degree, lo those many years
ago, I have to say that I never thought this was how I'd be
using it. In fact, I even had enough hours for two degrees
(don't ask . . . sixty-five-year plan). Some days working full
time and having an income—even considering the panty hose
and headaches of day care for my little cherubs—sounds good
in comparison to volunteer hell. But then, I remember that
we only pass through this life once, and even if all I get is the
occasional hug from someone else's kid in the lunchroom
(while nary a glance from my own), I'm there for my
children when they need me. Oh, who am I kidding? I will
never do cafeteria duty again as long as I live! Yes, you can
hold me to that.

So if you ever do have to serve lunch duty, just remember
these words for the person in charge, and you'll do just fine: "I
don't think that's in my contract." Delivered with a plastic
smile, how could they object? Oh, and remember to bring your
own WT apron from home, 'cuz where's the fun in wearing
that stupid polyester one that they give you there? Keep on
your toes here though, ladies. The Muffia are everywhere,
especially the lunchroom. And what better place for them to
eat you for lunch than the school cafeteria?!

White Trash Mom ROI ANALYSIS

High Visibility/High Volunteer Hours
No alcohol involved, no weekly meetings, no paperwork. No off-site work. Usual suspects make it more fun. Your kid sees you doing it. Pro: Concentrated volunteer hours; your child and their friends see you. You also get to spy on other kids and see how they really act when their parents aren't around. Con: Can be a tough gig if you have a mean lunchroom supervisor. It's also very noticeable if you don't show up. Proceed with caution.

LIBRARY AIDE

Time Required:	Two to four hours
Frequency Required:	One to four times a month
Visibility:	Medium to high

Tacky Princess COMMENTS

In my humblest of WT opinions, this is a sweet gig. If you set it up with the librarian so it coincides with your student's library day, you get to see your kid during school hours. You will have the opportunity to observe how your child interacts with his or her classmates outside of the regular classroom environment but not in a purely social environment either. Call me weird, but this is one of the best volunteer gigs out there.

The kids are (generally) on their best behavior, as they are expected to be quiet and respectful of the books and each other at all times. I especially enjoy helping out when the littlest ones visit the library because they are so cute, and they look up at me adoringly, as they should. Let's face it, my own kids have moved far beyond gazing at me with any sort of affection. I'm lucky to get the occasional nod when they see me in the halls at school. These days, in order to get a hug at school, I have to do volunteer duty during my youngest nephew's class period. Having him come barreling up to me, screaming my name, and embracing me in a child-size bear hug . . . well, it certainly adds to my enjoyment, to say the least! And the littlest kids still need help selecting books and will even take my advice.

When the students aren't visiting the library, duties include reshelving books, making new library displays, and taking inventory. I have to concede that if you don't like your librarian, this could be an entirely different experience. However, if your librarian is a treat like ours, or even tolerable, then I contend that this is one of the best-kept volunteering secrets out there. But don't tell anyone. We don't want everyone to know. Then, the posts might fill up too quickly. So, keep it on the down low, okay? Ix-nay on the atter-chay. Got it? Good.

 White Trash Mom ROI ANALYSIS

High Visibility/Low Volunteer Hours

No alcohol involved, no weekly meetings, no paperwork.

No off-site work. You can't talk in the library so it doesn't matter who you work with. Pro: Good ROI for the time spent. You get to spy on kids. Your child will see you do the job and that's a plus. Con: I disagree with TP completely on this. I was always in trouble as a kid in the library since I talked all the time. The library mafia must have a poster on me because all school librarians look at me with suspicion. I vote thumbs down on this one but it could work for you.

Room Parent (also known as Class Parent)

Time Required: two to three hours

Frequency Required: Once or twice per quarter (holiday parties)

Visibility: Very high

Tacky Princess COMMENTS

Once again, it is a joke, in my humble opinion, to refer to this post as Room Parent. In my eleven years as a school volunteer, I have never once seen a man's name on the list of "parents" who are room parents. Having said that, would it be waaaaaaay cool if a dad stepped up to the plate and volunteered to be a Room Parent? Or perhaps even a whole band of fathers? You bet it would. It could change the way we do parties. It could reverse the effects of global warming, for Pete's sake. I really think we might be on to something here. However, on second thought, I do believe that the women who run these school volunteer programs with an iron fist might just discourage this from transpiring. I don't know. Just a sneaking suspicion. A gut feeling. A gnawing reality, if you will, that it would take a great shake-up for dads to start running this time-honored tradition.

Having said all of the above, being a Room Mom is one of the best volunteer gigs out there. Very high visibility with the kids and not nearly as many hours to put in as one might think. A little bit of planning and creativity can go a long way with this one.

White Trash Mom ROI ANALYSIS

High Visibility/Low Volunteer Hours

No alcohol involved unless you drink before you go (not recommended). No weekly meetings and only minor paperwork. Some of the job is spent off-site but it's shopping, so that doesn't count. Pro: Usual suspects make it more fun. Your children see you in the classroom so this is one of the biggest reasons to do this job. At my younger daughter's school, Room Parent is the best gig of all. I try to sign up every year for Room Parent, as the job scares some moms due to the high visibility. The moms that are scared off are those who did not get the correct intel on this job. Being a Room Parent has the highest ROI Analysis in my neighborhood.

SCHOOL COMMITTEE (OR AN EXCUSE FOR HAPPY HOUR)

Time Required:	Twenty-five hours total for the year
Frequency Required:	Hours concentrated around an event or project
Visibility:	Low with children, high with school administrators

White Trash Mom's COMMENTS

This type of volunteering is my favorite way to volunteer my time at school. Committees can be an excellent way to combine socializing and volunteering if you and your crew of WT Mom friends all decide to volunteer for one event or project. Having a WT Mom "committee" is a great excuse to have a lot of "meetings" to plan the event or project. These meetings are usually held at night and these meetings are most effective if they are served with drinks.

 *White Trash Mom* ROI ANALYSIS

Medium Visibility/Medium Volunteer Hours
Combining fun and volunteer hours via "committee" work with other WT Moms is the ultimate in mom multitasking. While in the medium range of ROI, this method of volunteering is *high* in the area of fun.

Make sure you choose the right mix of WT Moms for the committee, so work actually gets done. WT Moms who must be part of your committee include:

- ❖ WT Mom who is good with finances, so the money for the committee is in order.
- ❖ WT Mom who can speak fluent "Muffia-speak" so that your committee is in contact with the Muffia queens who run the school.
- ❖ Salesperson WT Mom to pressure and cajole other parents to help your committee pull off your project.
- ❖ Expert "brown-nose" mom on the committee so that your event or project runs smoothly, with as little red tape as possible. This is the role that I usually serve, since sucking up to the teachers and administrators is my gift.

I've had good luck and many happy hours using the "committee" method of volunteering. Planning meetings can begin six to nine months before the even, giving a great excuse for lots of nights out with the girls. After all, it's for the kids, right?

Q AND A WITH TACKY PRINCESS,
VOLUNTEER ROI ANALYSIS EXPERT

WTM: What is your take on getting all your volunteer hours in one giant job? For example, what if you chaperone the class trip out of town or are in charge of the school musical?

TP: Generally speaking, you don't get the maximum ROI from such gigs. Yes, you get high visibility for that one job, but it's for a very short period. Many of the other jobs we've illustrated here have a far better ROI, in my opinion. Repeat assignments also offer the added advantage of being easy. Once you've done them once or twice, they're easy. Plain and simple. With a large project, it's like inventing the wheel, just figuring out how to do things. By the end of the project, you are swearing you'll never do it again, so there goes your easy factor. You may know how to do it, but you'd never be stupid enough to sign on for it again!

WTM: Room Parent gigs are very sweet, in my opinion. But what if I am paired with a "major mental case" or some other nightmare scenario?

TP: It's part of the risk you take when you sign up. There are going to be years when you have to face the MMC (major mental case). Hopefully, there will only be one of them, and the rest of the women assigned to the job can compensate for her crazy ways. And remember, dear, there is no such thing as a free ride. Even good jobs have a downside.

Warning from White Trash Mom on Volunteering in One Giant Job

I used the "giant job" volunteer philosophy for my older daughter's school last year. I volunteered to drive a class of seventh-graders on a class educational trip. Long hours of driving with teens, going to museums, and the giant ball of twine. By the end of the second day, I was completely postal. Later that evening, after dropping off the kids at our hotel and making sure the adult/kid ratio was manageable, another mom and I went out for an emergency beer at a local pub. The alcohol saved my life . . . and probably the lives of the children. Be sure to weigh it carefully before you volunteer for an overnight field trip. And be sure you know where you can get something to drink in an emergency.

WTM: What are the warning signs of an MMC?

TP: *One of the biggest red flags of a full-blown MMC is if the mom wants to have a meeting about something that doesn't need a meeting. For example, the mom wants to have an hour-long meeting to discuss the Halloween party.*

If the mom in question is a rookie, you can overlook this. But if the mom is an experienced veteran but needs a big powwow to plan an activity for a class party, you're in trouble.

WTM: Training rookie moms can be a difficult job, especially if the rookie mom has started on the path to "the dark side"

of the Muffia. Do you have any advice for how a White Trash Mom can help another mom see the light?

TP: *First of all, you need to remember that becoming trashy is each mother's choice. You can't force someone and you can't make a mom part of our White Trash Mom world if she's not ready. As hard as it is, sometimes you just need to watch the new moms fry.*

Recently, one of my White Trash Mom friends wrote me about a holiday party that involved two veteran White Trash Moms and a rookie mom. The new mom showed signs of moving toward the dark side, but there was still a chance to turn her.

The White Trash Moms tried as hard as they could to steer the rookie mom away from doing a messy craft during this holiday event. They gave her other suggestions and warned her of the hell that awaited her should she attempt to use a hot-glue gun in a room full of second-graders.

The rookie mom ignored their wise advice and went ahead with the craft. As a result, the second-graders ate her alive. One boy had to be sent home due to burns as a result of sticking the hot-glue gun up his nose on a dare. Another girl had to go to the nurse because she ate so much regular glue while she was waiting in line for the rookie mom to pass out the art materials.

It was painful. The rookie mom had to leave the party, covered in sparkly fairy dust, immediately after the craft portion while mumbling something about a doctor's appointment. However, when the next holiday party came around, the rookie entertained no thoughts of crafting. She even suggested a little drink after the party. She's on the right track.

The lesson here is that sometimes you have to use tough love and let the rookies find out for themselves how ugly it can get.

One Final Volunteer Note from Tacky Princess

When I went from being a full-time working mom to a stay-at-home mom, the word spread incredibly quickly that I was at home. Everyone figured that if I could swing being a working career mom all those years, I could handle the school volunteer jobs just great. There's just one catch. Moderation. Don't sign up for everything. Ease yourself in. And if you find you dislike a particular job, don't be afraid to relinquish it the following year. Also, keep in mind that when you sign up at the beginning of the school year, you are signing up for nine months of work. Nine months. The time it takes to manufacture one of your children. That's a pretty big commitment.

Volunteer ROI Analysis Wrap-Up

Follow the rules of "Volunteer ROI Analysis" and you will sail through the shark-infested waters of being a school volunteer. If you choose not to take our advice and want to do it your way, you may eventually suffer a burnout or get sucked into the volunteer abyss!

The bottom line is to pace yourself. Volunteering at school is a marathon that begins at the time you enter the major leagues of elementary school and lasts until your child graduates high school. Don't overbook yourself and don't let people guilt you into doing more than you can. Most of all, keep the important Volunteer ROI Analysis in mind as you consider each job.

8

Fakin' It for
the Bake Sale

Home-baked items are an extremely important measurement of your performance as a mother. From Fresno to Philly, you will automatically be labeled as a bad mother if you bring store-bought treats to school. This is the gospel at every school.

You Are What You Bake

The baked goods and treats you bring to your child's school will be judged by the Muffia and by the other mothers. As silly as it sounds, you are what you bake. I don't make the rules, campers, I only give you the truth. Your baked goods are under a microscope and you need to make the right impression, because it impacts your child. Everything you do, every cookie you bring to school . . . it affects your son or daughter.

The Birthday Party Example

It is your child's birthday party and they are celebrating at school. You are responsible for bringing the birthday treat. Dig, if you will, why "you are what you bake" in the eyes of the school community: See chart on following page.

Never bring stuff right out of the box. You are just asking for trouble.

This standard for home baking is insane, right? Welcome to the reality of modern motherhood. You might not like what I am telling you but I'm not wrong. We all know that homemade treats taste better than boxed goods. In a perfect world, everyone would have time to bake perfect cookies. You will notice the word "perfect" twice in that last sentence, and if perfect is in the air, the dreaded Muffia can't be far behind.

Baked Goods and the Muffia

The evil Muffia use home-baked goods as a way to prove their superiority and perfection. Appearing thoughtful and perfect are missions of the Muffia. There is nothing that the self-proclaimed perfect mothers love more than bringing in a homemade apple strudel for teacher appreciation week and then telling everyone they "whipped it up" with "no trouble" the night before. (You *know* they were finishing the icing at 2 A.M.)

How to Cheat the "Home-Baked Rule"

If you don't love to bake or you don't have time to bake, I am here to tell you the White Trash Mom Method of cheating the Home-Baked Rule of being a perfect mother.

BAKED GOODS FOR PARTY	MESSAGE YOU SEND
Store-bought cupcakes. Brought in store packaging with price tag on it.	I don't have time to cook. Which means I don't have time for my child. Which means I am a bad mother.
Fancy gourmet cookies with every child's name on every cookie. It's clear you purchased the cookies and paid a small fortune for them.	I want to impress everyone. I am a social climber and I have too much money. I am a bad mother because I would rather throw money at a problem instead of baking something at home.
Home-baked cupcakes.	I did not overdo it and I am not trying to impress people with my baked goods. I am a good mother because I baked.
Fake-Baked Cake (via WTM's recipe).	I did not overdo it and I am not trying to impress people with my baked goods. I am a good mother because I baked.
Toll House "Slice and Bake Cookies."	I don't have time to cook so I half-assed tried to pass off home-baked cookies. I am lazy and I am trying to cheat.
Cookies from a box brought in for the party. No attempt to disguise the fact these are boxed cookies.	I don't even try to play the game. I openly disregard your rules and think they are silly. I am a rebel.

Using my method, you do *not* bake the cake . . . you buy it at the store and then decorate it, put it on a platter, and *pretend* you made it. The White Trash Mom Method of Fake-Baking is very simple and it is a far more efficient use of time than either:

1. Spending two hours baking something for your kids to take to school that will taste like drywall because you are, at your core, a really bad cook.
2. Feeling guilty and giving the Muffia something to talk about because you gave your kid a Sara Lee coffee cake to bring for the teachers' luncheon instead of the perfectly cooked desserts that the Muffia members served up.

HOW TO "BAKE" A STORE-BOUGHT CAKE

Nothing is more fun than to beat the Muffia at their own game. Just follow the "recipe" below for the White Trash Mom way to bring treats to school:

Step One—"Oh, Sh** " Moment

Insert your favorite expletive here. Of course, you *forgot* that you were supposed to bring a treat/birthday cake to your child's class or activity. You remember at the last minute or one of your WT Mom friends calls to remind you. You race to the store.

Step Two—"Baking" Your Instant Cake

Buy a plain white unfrosted store-bought cake. These
can be found in the baked goods area of your grocery store. If you don't see a plain white cake,
beg the people behind the counter to give you
one. I have found that crying is often helpful. Remember, you are doing this for your kids.

Step Three—Collect Your Decorations

Go to the aisle of the store where the cake-decorating stuff is.
Get *frosting in a can* to decorate the cake. Also buy the coolest
stuff you can find for the top of the cake. Race to the candy aisle
and grab some candy to throw on the cake. As you all know,
candy is like a drug to children. Nothing makes them happier
than to mainline some sugar.

Step Four—Replate Your Cake

This is a crucial step in the home-baked deception. Go home
and take the cake out of the store pan! Put the cake on either a
cake platter or a disposable serving dish. See below for details on
each method of fake food presentation.

Cake-Platter Method

Put the cake on a $9.99 cake platter from Target or Kmart. If you
are not a veteran of the "Muffia wars" and you do not have your

own personal serving dish, go buy one now—*before* you need one. Trust me. All the perfect mothers have cake platters. Just watch any 1960s television sitcom if you doubt me.

Disposable-Serving-Tray Method

If you have loaned out your cake platter to another mom or have not yet made it out to get the cake platter for your WT Mom Fake Cake, use a disposable pan. Get one with a lid that is big enough for your cake. You can get this at the store along with other "ingredients" for your "cake baking."

Step Five—Imperfect Decoration

After replating your cake, begin decorating it. Be sure to make it look less than perfect. You *want* it to look that way because most home-baked goods *are*. After making sure the icing is a little bit uneven, sprinkle (or throw) the candy on top in a fun fashion. Create a wonderful and whimsical cake!

Step Six—Lie Through Your Teeth

Take the cake to school and swear that it is a homemade little recipe that you got from Great-Aunt Mitsy. Never admit that the cake is store-bought. No matter how much pressure the Muffia apply, *do not crack*.

Guilt and Stupidity

Faking a cake may seem stupid, and it's dishonest to pretend to bake a cake. Why go through all the trouble? Why not just bring in

Important Disclaimer about Disposable-Dish Fake-Cake Presentation

Be sure to look the Muffia square in the eyes as you tell them that you brought a disposable dish because it's "less trouble for everybody." Act like you are doing them a favor . . . *because you care.* Like driving a stake through the heart of a vampire, using the sweet and thoughtful reason that you brought the disposable dish will make their Muffia moms' little tar hearts just melt with envy. The Muffia spend their lives trying to prove their superiority and it makes them tired. They will hate you for the disposable-tray idea because they didn't think of it first. The Muffia women are all about how they can look beautiful—they are completely pulled together—and they can bake lemon bars to die for. Because baking is one of the core parts of showing perfection, anything you can do to outshine the Muffia beasts in baking is a blow to them.

a box of Hostess Twinkies or cookies or something? Well, if the other moms bring home-baked, and you're the only one who doesn't, your kid will notice. And the Muffia will make your life miserable. Look, they needed a cake and they got a cake. Your kid's happy. The Muffia is off your back until the next bake sale. Everybody wins. It's one of the little white lies that keeps society going.

Fake-Baking Works

I promise you. I have done the fake-cake thing zillions of times over my White Trash Mom career. It has saved me hours of baking bad cakes, cookies, brownies, and more. I've succeeded at really bugging some of the Muffia by bringing baked goods that rival their creations.

Now put your guilt away and let's read how to "make" other fake foods for school. Our next session will deal with how to make store-purchased brownies look and taste like homemade.

WHITE TRASH MOM'S
FAUX CARAMEL BROWNIES

Step One—Forgetting You Had to Do It

You forgot *again*. As usual, you race to the store at the last minute.

Step Two—Seek Out the Baked Goods Aisle

If your supermarket has a bakery, go there first. In most grocery stores over by the doughnuts and cakes, there is usually an area that has already baked brownies. There are not very many of these brownies in 8×8-inch pans (I suspect the Muffia is on to me), but they are there if you look for them. Buy two pans of brownies. Do not pass go. Do not stop and read *People* magazine. Focus.

Step Three—Go to the Baking Aisle

Go to the baking aisle of the store. Purchase either of the following:

1. Caramel squares
2. Caramel sauce, if you can find it

Step Four—Purchase a Disposable Plate

For the Faux Caramel Brownies recipe, I use the disposable plate 100 percent of the time.

It's too difficult to have a "special brownie pan" on hand and besides that, if you go too far with the fake pans, you might get busted. It is for this reason and the fact that my ADD brain can't remember too many things that I always use disposable pans for Faux Brownies. See step four in the Fake Cake recipe for more information about disposable pans.

Step Five—Mash and Smush

Rush home from the store. Put the brownies into the disposable pan. If there is icing, make sure the icing side is on top. Next, melt the caramel squares or the caramel sauce in the microwave. Then get a big spoon and put "dollops" of caramel on top of the brownies in a very random and inconsistent way. Use no pattern and do not make it neat. You want it to be very messy on top. After putting the caramel on the brownies, take a fork and smush the sides of the brownies a little. Use the "Fork Smush" in different places around the brownies, again with no discernible pattern.

Step Six—Cut with Dull Knife

After preparing the brownies, get out a very dull knife. Proceed to cut the brownies in a very uneven way. Make sure that the brownies vary in size.

There is nothing that screams store-bought like brownies that are of uniform size. Make little ones and some that are extra large. Take a brief moment to step back and admire your genius.

Step Seven—Lie, Lie, Lie

Take the brownies to school and swear that you whipped them up while working on your quilt last night. As with the cake recipe (and all of WTM's fake food), you cannot disclose the true recipe.

MORE SUGGESTIONS FOR FAKE-BAKING TIPS

Toll House Ready-Made Cookie Dough

Buy the Toll House Cookie Dough that is ready-made and can be found in the refrigerated dough section. Mush the dough into a square or rectangular bake pan and bake for the time indicated on the box. Let cool, add frosting or caramel to the top, cut into bars, and then dump the cookies onto either a disposable plate or cake platter (so it is more of a cookie "bar"). Take to school and lie like a rug.

Big disclaimer on the baking thing. I have friends who are not card-carrying members of the Muffia and are true-blue White Trash Moms, who are excellent cooks.

These women love to bake and are damn good at it. One of my very best friends in the world and the godmother of my oldest daughter can whip up cookies or brownies without blinking an eye. There is nothing wrong with baking and loving it.

There *is* something wrong with assuming that anyone who doesn't bring home-baked goods to school events is somehow lacking a mother gene. But we aren't going to change the standard of perfect motherhood and baking, so we'll fake it.

Holiday Cookies

Holidays are particularly vexing because this is when the Muffia come out in big numbers with their home-baked holiday cookies. Plain sugar cookies can be purchased pretty easily at the grocery store at the last minute. How do I know this? Because I have done it for years and it works.

Purchase the holiday cookies and then some canned icing. Decorate with candy or sprinkles. Take to school in a fun and disposable holiday festive plate.

Experience that warm feeling of happiness as the Muffia mothers in your homeroom glare at you.

Cookin' with the White Trash Mom

In an appendix for this book, you'll find other excellent WT Mom recipes and tips. You are what you bake, so a little bit of effort and creativity can go a long way.

After-School Activities for
the White Trash Family

The many activities that are available to our children will be no
surprise to anyone with even a thimbleful of knowledge regarding parenting. The endless activities list comes with a lot of
problems:

- ❖ Parents are sucking the life out of our kids by not letting the kids have a minute's peace.
- ❖ WT families love a good game but organized sports
  can take over the whole family, not to mention the
  neighborhood.
- ❖ Kids aren't always the ones who want all their time
  filled. I'll give you one guess as to who wants all the
  time filled. Okay, I'll give you a hint, it's spelled M-U-
  F-F-I-A!
- ❖ When Mommy and Daddy scream on the sidelines it's
  no wonder that little junior sporty is a terror on and
  off the field.

"IF YOU CAN'T COME IN ON SATURDAY, DON'T BOTHER COMING IN ON SUNDAY"

The above saying is popular in the ad agency business. The ad agency business requires a seven-day workweek and this phrase sums up the crazy hours agency people put in to be successful. I am reminded of this phrase as I think about my kids' after-school activities because the same mentality exists. There is unspoken pressure to get your child into sports as early as possible—even if the child is not ready to try the sport—because your child will get left behind if you wait even a year. You think I'm kidding? Here is an example that actually happened to one of my friends!

At her daughter's school, the parents formed a soccer team for her daughter's first-grade class. Her daughter chose not to play in first grade but the next year the little girl wanted to try it. My WTM friend called the mother who organized the team in first grade and here is the conversation:

> WTM: "My daughter wants to play soccer this year, how do I sign her up?"
> DIVA SOCCER MOM: "Well . . . she didn't play *last year* . . ."
> WTM: "What?"
> DIVA SOCCER MOM: "If she didn't play *last year*, I'm afraid it's going to be hard to play this year, she's kind of behind . . ."

According to the Diva of soccer, my friend's daughter was "out" as far as trying soccer. In second grade, at age seven, she was washed-up! Lucky for my friend, there were many sane parents at the school. When my WT Mom pal told the other parents about the phone call and being "washed-up" in second grade, these parents rebelled against the Diva mom. The Diva mother's attempt to shut out kids after first grade was silly. Several of the parents left the Diva's team and formed another team that was open to all girls who wanted to play.

TYPES OF ACTIVITIES AND THEIR POTENTIAL EFFECTS ON OUR KIDS

Moderation is the key to sanity with after-school activities for kids. If all your family's time together is spent in a car going to a game, you might need to cut down on the number of activities the kids participate in. After all, what meaning does life have if you can't take time to go through the drive-thru as a family, then watch a trashy TV program?

1. Sports—Can be a huge problem for children of all ages (and the parents who coach them, er, raise them).
2. Other Activities—Generally speaking, they're great, as long as you don't overdo it. Don't enroll them in oil painting, cooking, and dancing classes all at once.
3. Playdates—Tread carefully here. Taking your children to homes of the Muffia can be dangerous business.

First let's look at a few of the most popular children's activities. When you read through the following list, I want you to see which activities jump out when you think of overprogrammed, overstimulated children. Let's just give this a try:

Ballet/Dancing/ Music Lessons	Basketball	Choir
Baseball	Tumbling	Volleyball
Horseback Riding	Karate	Science Club
Gymnastics	Swimming	Running/Track
Soccer	Cub Scouts/Boy Scouts	Drama Club
Brownies/Girl Scouts	Ice Skating	Dance/ Cheerleading
Art Classes	Youth Group	Football

I'm going to bet the activities that you marked have to do mostly with sports. Am I right, or am I right? Some would argue that dance fits into the sports category, and that may well be. You could also argue that many other activities can get a little out of hand.

Children and their sporting activities have taken over the lives of many families I know. While some find great pleasure in this (yes, they really do), others find it to be a tremendous drain, both on their wallets and their leisure time. Somehow, we are kidding ourselves that it's for our kids' own good—in their best interest. But is it really?

Not every child is going to play sports in high school. And *very* few of them will play in college. A comparatively *minuscule* number of them will play professionally. In fact, chances are pretty good that they'll sooner win your state's lottery. So why are we so wrapped up in these sports?

Pressure of Elementary- and Middle-School Sports

As your child gets older, the pressure mounts to compete. And if your child is in any way, shape, or form talented at sports— *double ouch!* Both on the wallet and the time. The problem is that at the point when many of these children get to high school, they are already so burned out on sports, they're not even interested in going out for their high school team. And you've spent the last six years or so traveling from town to town, tournament to tournament, shelling out every last dollar you had to support this "love," this "drive," this "obsession." It's become clear that some of the parents want it more than kids!

I can't begin to count the number of times a kid on a court or field makes a goal or a big play and immediately looks up into the stands for parental approval. And this goes on well into the middle-school years and even into high school. That's sad. The kids are doing it as much for their parents' sake as for their own.

What's a White Trash Mom to Do?

If your son or daughter really loves sports, let 'em play, but if it's a longing for *your* glory days or keeping up with the Muffia that's driving you to practice after practice and game after game, then read the following WTM's fully approved activity guide.

Scouts

For my money, Girl Scouts and Boy Scouts offer a great way for kids to be in a noncompetitive environment and just be a kid. Kids learn to respect others, how to get along in a group setting, and that life isn't all about money and sports. Because each child only antes up a certain amount of money at the beginning of each school year, Scouts learn that they have to live within a budget. And through various activities like trips to a nursing home, campouts, and selling cookies or trash bags (I know . . . groan . . .) they learn to give back to their community. These are valuable lessons.

Music Lessons

Now, I may sound a little off my WT rocker on this one, but bear with me. In my humble opinion, music lessons give children balance and a sense of structure in an otherwise chaotic environment. Music lessons keep my kids from egging the neighbors' houses. And I have to have something to chat with the Muffia about, right?

Martial Arts

Karate, Tae kwon do, and judo seem to give a lot of kids a great sense of pride. They also seem to be a "sports endeavor" that doesn't involve hype over who is the best, etc. Research has shown that martial arts training is an excellent choice for children with ADHD. It helps instill a sense of self-esteem and self-discipline. Kids of all shapes and sizes appear to do well with karate, judo, and Tae kwon do, so I am in full support of these.

Art

Art is a way to express emotions and is an outlet for kids to gain confidence in their abilities. The kids that don't excel in the traditional school subjects can really shine in art. Drawing, painting, graphic design, even creating movies on video cameras can be an invaluable way for kids to shine.

Tennis Is a WT Sport

If your child has not had success in team sports, sign up for tennis. Tennis is a game that doesn't have the pressure of the team and is a way to be successful in sports without being part of a team. You don't need a country club to play; the public courts near you will do just fine. The best part of tennis is that it's a sport that can be played for life. Unlike soccer or basketball, people play tennis all the way through adulthood. I completely stink at tennis but I have fun playing it and I've made my girls sign up.

Get Back to Nature

Getting outside is great for kids. If your kids show an interest in nature or animals, *find a way to get them involved* and learn more. There are groups and organizations that nurture a love of nature and/or animals. One of my daughter's friends is crazy about animals and there's a program that lets teenagers help at the local animal shelters. Let them keep bug collections and make an effort to show them nature. If you don't have a lot of green in your community, go to a museum or science exhibit. Going for a hike is up there with a root canal for me (as is camping) but my older daughter L-O-V-E-S to go, so we go and get out there. I just make sure my iPod is working and I have TiVoed the latest episode of *Project Runway* to watch when I get back from the great outdoors.

WHITE TRASH HOUSEHOLD AND FRIENDS

When you allow your child to go over to a friend's house, you are letting them out of the safety of your White Trash Haven. Where your child will discover that Commando is *not* practiced by other children, that Twinkies are not an acceptable breakfast food, and you must prep them for encountering values and ideas that do not match your WT household. If you don't prepare your kids, it can truly be a harrowing experience for both of you.

White Trash Mom Household vs. a "Normal" Household

When my daughters visit the neighbors, they do normal things.

- ❖ Make fudge.
- ❖ Play board games or PlayStation 2.
- ❖ Watch DVDs.
- ❖ Do art projects.

Conversely, when they come to our house, the activities are a little different:

❖ Make a video where the dolls get beheaded and Trailer Trash Turleen (see chapter 10) is taken away by aliens.
❖ Dress the pug dogs up in bikinis and parade them around the neighborhood.
❖ See if they can get the dogs to "pee" in the toilet.
❖ Make a fort out of an inflatable swimming pool and Slip 'n' Slide that are still outside from last summer even though it's February.

You see my point. So, I'd like to offer you some pointers for how to prepare your son or daughter when going for a playdate (especially if you know in advance that the playdate is in Muffia territory).

Tips for Your White Trash Prodigy's OOTTP (Out of the Trailerpark Playdate)

1. Wear underwear (commando is highly overrated in this situation).
2. Do not bring the beheaded Ken doll or Trailer Trash Turleen (see chapter 10).
3. Make it a point to feed the little monster a healthy breakfast and/or lunch that day. Otherwise, it will invariably transpire that you feed him a Twinkie and Kool-Aid for breakfast (again), and this can only do damage for you in your new Muffia relationship.
4. Bathing the night before is highly advisable.
5. Check your little cherub's pockets before the playdate, as there is no telling what he or she might take out of the safety of your White Trash Haven.
6. There's no sense now in trying to indoctrinate your

WT prodigy about the evil ways of the Muffia. You'll just have to trust that the WT values that you've in-stilled at home will somehow come shining through. Yes, I know it's hard, but it's all you can do.

7. I repeat: Wear underwear. Check now. You can't be too careful on this one when in enemy territory.

8. If you possibly can, have a dinner the night before where the whole family sits down at the table. No *American Idol*. No *Desperate Housewives*. No *Project Runway*. Hide the take-out boxes from the kids, so they think you cooked it. Take the meal out of the oven as they come into the kitchen to eat. They'll remember this and share the story at their play-date the next day. You'll score major points over the microwave burritos you were planning to serve again—trust me.

9. If your younger child wants to bring a toy to share, be sure to perform a "security" check on what that item is.

10. Don't be late for school the morning of the playdate. (Yes, I speak from experience. "I got my fourth tardy this week. Mrs. O'Flaherty says that if I get one more, that'll be a record!")

Let's Recap

Sports: *Take a Chill Pill* (see the White Trash Mom Glossary). It's 99.99999 percent likely that your child will not go pro. It's 95 percent likely that your child will not even play in college. Keep it in perspective, folks.

he National Anthem—Advanced

dvanced students who have mastered burping the na-
em, learn the best way to humiliate your family with
rping at mass or at family reunions with lots of elderly

FOR PARENTS ONLY

lock Somewhere

ws parents how to take any volunteer situation and
arty, usually involving alcohol. Need to sort lunch
's a special tonight at the Gaf Irish Pub. Need to
ting Committee meeting? Laminating goes so well
s! Class ends with a party.

Other Activities: Take it easy. Buzzing your kid from one activity to the next isn't fun for anyone. And really, isn't *fun* the overall point? That, and having a well-rounded kid?

Friends: Proceed with caution, and do your best to ensure that
that any Muffia children don't see too much of the inner WTM.
With any luck, you'll come off as quirky and offbeat instead of
the insane White Trash Mother/queen that you are.

Ask your other White Trash Mom friends in the field to
learn how they handle children's activities. You should be using
each other as a sounding board and idea exchange. We have to
stick together. We are a movement. We are united. Hear us roar.

AFTER-SCHOOL ACTIVITIES—IN
THE REAL WORLD

Here are some of the suggestions for activities that *should* be offered:

How to Write a Seventh-Grade Term Paper (For Parents)

This after-school class should be mandated for parents of fifth-
graders and older to help with the term papers. Since some of the
term papers that are assigned to children are completely insane
in terms of expectations, it is assumed that when such papers are
given, the parents will help with the work. One of my WTM pals
had to help her sixth-grader with a paper that required—and I am
not kidding—thirty-six different sources as reference.

Make a Million Dollars Using Change from Your Parents

Excellent class for children to learn how to make money through the change given to them via parents. Your dad gives you a $10 bill for milk. You buy the $2 gallon of milk—and keep the rest. Various tactics of confusion, distraction, and magic will allow you to make over $100 a month or more . . . just by keeping the change.

Chinese Water Torture and You

For students. Using the drip-drip-drip method made popular by the Chinese, this class shows you how to relentlessly get your way simply by breaking your parents down until they let you do what you want.

Professional Shopping 101

For mothers and daughters. Excellent training for moms and their girls on how to execute the perfect postshopping cover-up. Course includes ways to sneak home the bags from Nordstrom, how to combine bags from various stores, and how to wear new clothes without the clothes looking like new. Great prep for daughters to use when they are married.

HOW ABOUT SOME I[...]
THAT THEY COUL[...]
IN THEIR D[...]

Eye Rolling for Teens

How to effectively roll your ey[...]
when asked to perform mund[...]
house. Learn to add the prope[...]
at family events.

Walk Away Quickly

Learn how to successfully [...]
but deadly" fart. Topics in [...]
brother or sister.

Importance of Blame

It doesn't matter what [...]
This class will show yo[...]
almost anything.

Pushing Their Butto[...]

Learn the latest tools [...]
maximum return on [...]

Burping t[...]

For those a[...]
tional anth[...]
your gift: b[...]
relatives.

It's Five O'c[...]

This class sho[...]
turn it into a [...]
tickets? There[...]
have a Lamina[...]
with margarita[...]

10

Your Children Will Be in Therapy . . . Get Used to It

One of the central realities about being a WTM is that your children *will* be in therapy eventually. It really does not matter what you do because something that you do to your children will drive them to a therapist's couch. And you, the mother, will be blamed. Because, as we all know, it is always the mother's fault. From Freud to Anthony Perkins in *Psycho*, everything is blamed on the mother. It is a fact of life, ladies, so the sooner you realize this, the sooner you can relax and accept it.

Your kids will need to see a shrink because of the following reasons:

- ❖ Things You Say to Your Kids—Momisms
- ❖ Things You Do to and for Your Kids
- ❖ The Experts

Things You Say to Your Kids—Momisms

A "normal" mother may beat herself up for the outrageous pronouncements, threats, and rants that she throws at her kids. A White Trash Mom knows that such ranting is completely insane and you will laugh about it later. But rest assured that your momisms will be therapy fodder at a rate of $150 per hour later on.

You know you are a mom when you say things to your children that you swore you would never allow to cross your lips. You know what I am talking about—those phrases that your mom said to you and as a kid you thought to yourself, *I will never say that to my children* . . . but then you did. Here is an example of one of my momisms. Multiply the story below by one thousand and you will know exactly why my girls will be seeing a shrink. I hope what I have done to my little princesses makes you feel better about what you've said to your kids. If not, it's never too early to make an appointment with the local shrink.

Momism #548

Here's my worst momism, which I yelled at my children during Lenten season in 2005.

I was dragging the girls to mass. As we were speeding toward the church (almost late, as per usual) I was on the phone with one of my best friends. We grew up together and her mother used to drive the car and then scream at us to behave while she whacked us with her house slipper. It was a soft house slipper but I think you get the picture.

Anyway, while speeding to mass I was talking to my friend on the cell phone and yelling at my kids. Nice, huh? A picture-perfect Catholic family.

Anyway, so one of the girls says something like: "I don't want to go to church, Moooooom. I don't feel like it . . . ."

To which I reply: "Do you think that Jesus wanted to die on the cross? Do you think that he felt like it?" (Please note—it was totally a reflex from that mom gene, it was not really me talking, I swear.)

In my yelling, I forgot my friend was on the phone. She will *never* let me live it down. Being such longtime friends, she has also told most of our other twisted friends so that they make fun of me as well. I can take comfort in the fact that comments like the above will be brought up later by my daughters with their future therapy appointments.

The White Trash Mom blog is an excellent way to connect with other White Trash Moms. I always get great advice and laughs from my WTM readers.

After I wrote about my momism moment I was flooded with comments from readers about the stuff they say to their children. There were far too many great comments to include them all in this book but here are a few of my favorite momisms from my friends and "sisters" in White Trash:

❖ Quit whining. You could be in India with flies around your eyes.
❖ You can't give up God for Lent.
❖ Did you know that Jesus *and* Santa are watching you? They are both watching and they don't like what they see.

❖ When you break your head open, you're going to have to clean up your own blood, I swear!

❖ Quit climbing! I'm not taking you to the emergency room tonight! If you break a bone you will have to wait until tomorrow to get help.

❖ Don't come running and crying to me after you break your legs!

Here are some of my childhood favorites that I swore would never pass my lips . . . but somehow they did:

❖ If I have to stop this car ONE MORE TIME . . .

❖ I am not the maid! (cruise director, activity director . . .)

❖ No one is touching *anyone* in this house *ever* again!

❖ No one is ever talking to *anyone* in this house *ever* again!

❖ I swear to God I will take that————away until hell freezes over!

❖ If you know what's good for you, you won't————.

❖ I am on my last nerve!

❖ You've ruined this nice————for your sister. I hope you're happy.

Things You Do to and for Your Kids

As a mom you try to do the best you can. You try to trust your instincts and your values to do what you can to make your kids into productive and wonderful humans. As a WT Mom you realize that some of the things we do to our kids and for our kids will be the things they have issues with later in life. A WT Mom accepts she can't be perfect and that it doesn't matter what you do. If you work "outside the home," your kids will have issues that you did not stay home with them. They will say you did not give them enough attention.

If you "don't work" (ha!) and stay home with the children, your kids will say that you did not provide them with enough "space" . . . you smothered them too much by being around all the time. If you work out of your home, you may run into the same issues.

My point is that your kids *will have issues* no matter what you do or how you raise them. So you need to be sure that you are raising the little humans the way you feel is best for them. Let me give you a few examples from my own little trailerpark:

Example #1—The *Thriller* Dance

If you want to strike terror into the hearts of my daughters, just turn on Michael Jackson's *Thriller*. They will break into a cold sweat because I actually know the dance steps to the entire *Thriller* music video. And I'm not afraid to do it.

Background

Knowing the dance steps to the *Thriller* video could be one of the biggest things I retained from my four years at college. I learned it as part of a college musical, at the height of the popularity of the *Thriller* video.

The Reason Thriller Will Send My Kids into Therapy

I have used my knowledge of Jackson's music video as a way of threatening my daughters to behave well. If they start to sass me too much or bring on a huge attitude in the presence of their friends, I threaten them with a lively-sounding offer:

"Hey, girls—did you know that I know all the steps to the *Thriller* dance? Want me to show you?"

My girls are instantly horrified . . . with good reason. I have actually started doing the dance with a little help from my friend Señor Patron (Patron Tequila) on summer nights. It's sad and rather pathetic but very fun for me.

White Trash Mom's Perspective on *Thriller* Dance

The way I see it, embarrassing my children is a given as a mother. By the simple fact I am their mother, I will make them cringe. When the girls D-I-E because of my dancing, I just tell them it's either the *Thriller* dance or something else, equally as embarrassing. It's the law.

Example #2—Tire Sale Summer

When I worked full time I had a job that required me to travel quite a bit.

Background

One summer, I dragged the girls all over the United States going to tire sale events. My clients loved it. My girls could sell tires to anyone! That summer it became very clear that the girls had inherited my dad's ability to sell "snow to Eskimos."

The Reason Tire Sales Will Send My Kids into Therapy

My girls can make an easy hundred dollars selling Kool-Aid in front of our house. Seriously. They are completely relentless. Whether it's a Kool-Aid stand or selling Girl Scout cookies, if they have you in their sights, just get out your wallet.

I am not exaggerating when I tell you that the sixth- and seventh-grade basketball-game concession-stand profits increase substantially when my older daughter is working behind the counter.

I probably have ruined any chance the girls had for a career in the nonprofit sector due to the fact that their sales abilities were honed and used at such an early age.

White Trash Mom's Perspective on Tire Sales

My kids are definitely warped by my work experiences. But I figure if I am going to warp them, it's better to do so knowing the value of making a dollar and how to work hard. Learning how to sell stuff will always help you later in life.

Example #3—Miss Minnesota

I allowed my daughter to dress up like a beauty queen for Halloween.

Background

My younger daughter wanted to be *Miss Minnesota* for Halloween. Why? No freaking idea. We are neither from Minnesota nor do we have a large family from that great state.

Shopping for the Miss Minnesota dress almost got me arrested. You should have seen the looks I got. Faster than you can say JonBenét Ramsey—the sales clerks are tag-teaming me in the store—one trying to get me *out* of their shop while the other one attempts to "hotline" me to Child Services.

I went searching online in an attempt *not* to have Child Services come to my door, wondering why I want an evening-gown getup for size 6x. It is on the Internet that I discovered pageant wear for children. Just talking about the online beauty-queen-dress stores gives me the chills so I'm not going there.

The Reason Miss Minnesota Will Send My Younger Daughter into Therapy

I found a cheap Christmas dress at Target that I kind of cut up a bit to look like a trampy beauty-pageant dress for a forty-eight-pound girl. I dressed her up like a hooker with a sash and even have the pictures to prove it. I'm sure these pictures will be part of her tell-all book twenty years from now—*Growing up with a White Trash Mom*—as well as setting her up for years of therapy.

White Trash Mom's Perspective on Miss Minnesota

I dressed my seven-year-old up like a hooker . . . on purpose. This will come back to haunt me later in life. My rationalization is that hopefully walking in high heels and tight skirts at a tender age will make it *not* as appealing when she gets older. I will keep you posted on this one. I'm not hopeful.

Example #4—White Trash Palace

I used to have an online retail store called White Trash Palace. Along with T-shirts and jeans, the shop sold a number of "kitschy" items online. I no longer have the store or sell the kitschy items but there are still remnants of this part of my life in our home. One of the items I sold was a doll called Trailer Trash Turleen. Turleen was one of my best sellers. You push her tummy and she says things like:

- ❖ "There's a twister comin'!"
- ❖ "Pour me a double. I'm drinkin' fer two!"
- ❖ "Burp!"

Background

My elder daughter makes movies. One day she had some friends over and they needed additional "action" figures for a movie and I told her she could use one of the Turleen dolls in the garage. As soon as I made the offer, I saw her face. She was horrified. But it gets worse because one of her friends says, "Oh, you gave my mom and dad one of those dolls. But they said that I couldn't play with it because it's not appropriate for kids."

The Reason Turleen Will Send My Kids Into Therapy

It's a safe bet that pregnant white trash dolls hanging around the house is not the norm. I am 99.9 percent sure that this will be coming back to haunt me as my older daughter talks to her therapist.

White Trash Mom's Perspective on Turleen

As a side note, the movie my daughter and her friends made that day is extremely clever and funny. They added alien invasions and a host of other great side plots for an excellent movie.

Example #5—Country and Western Songs

My girls could sing the words to "Goodbye Earl" by the Dixie Chicks back when one was six and the other was two. Two kinds of music play on my CD player regularly: Country. And Western.

Background

Not many other moms know the words to Jerry Jeff Walker's "Up Against the Wall Redneck Mother." Nor do many of the other suburban mothers know the history behind the George Jones classic "He Stopped Loving Her Today." I play other music of course, but C&W music is a staple in my car and in my house.

The Reason My C&W Songs Will Send My Kids Into Therapy

The hit movie *Walk the Line* about Johnny Cash and June Carter Cash made classic C&W music very hip again. But since my girls have had to listen to Johnny Cash's "Boy Named Sue" since they were babies, they parted ways with their buddies who suddenly loved Johnny Cash. I know that I have sung Waylon Jennings's "Lukenbach, Texas" one too many times for it not to warp the girls.

White Trash Mom's Perspective on Country and Western Songs

My Country and Western songs are in the "given" category. From my twisted view, children hate their parents' music. If a parent listens to the music, it is *uncool*. Therefore, I could listen to very hip music and they would still think I'm a dork. It is a given that I will be a dork, no matter what I do, as I am their mother. That is why I listen to the music I like and let the chips fall . . .

Example #6—White Trash Mom's Blog and Book

As I write this book and my blog, I know that my writing will be just one more reason my children will need therapy.

Background

Having a mother who calls herself White Trash Mom does not put me in the June Cleaver school of motherhood.

The Reason The White Trash Mom Handbook *Will Send My Kids into Therapy*

My children are twisted enough not to be too upset by The White Trash Mom Handbook. But I am certain that given enough time on a therapist's couch, a psychologist will definitely tell them that this has warped them for life and beyond.

White Trash Mom's Perspective on *The White Trash Mom Handbook*

I figure my kids will be slightly warped by my writing *before they have children*. But after they have children they will realize how insane motherhood can be and they will thank me.

Or at least they will forgive me.

What's a Mother to Do?

You have your own special things that will drive your kids to the shrink. You potty-trained them too late ... or too early. You used too much bad language or they walked in on you and your husband while you were playing "French Maid." The difference between WT Mothers and the rest of the world is that we know that our kids will be on the couch no matter what we do so we just try to do the best we can.

Your Kids Will Be in Therapy Because of "The Experts"

Besides the stuff you say to your kids and the stuff you do to your kids, there is one more piece of the puzzle that will ensure therapy for your children. Every few years there is a new "hot" expert that tells everyone how to raise his or her children. There are trends in child-rearing "experts" just as there are trends in everything else.

What used to be good for your little muffin's self-esteem is damaging to her psyche now. According to a recent study, it's bad to put kids in day care. But last year there was a study that said staying home with your kids was not as good as sending them to day care.

It's you—the mom—against an army of experts who are M.D.s, Ph.D.s, and other letters that are important. Unlike most mothers, the WT Mom realizes that she will screw up her child somehow. It's a given for WT Moms that their kids will be in therapy . . . it's just a matter of when and for how long. WT Moms don't need any expert help.

According to my WT scientific calculations it seems like there is a new "expert" on children every three years.

❖ Will your toddler be scarred for life by late-potty training?
❖ Will your son be gay if you let him play with dolls?
❖ Will your daughter turn into a bimbo if you let her play with Barbie dolls?

One expert says "yes," the other says "no." A WT Mom says, "Who knows? I'll deal with whatever happens when it happens. Pass the Velveeta."

Your Quirks Are Good Enough

Your neurotic quirks are just as good as any child psychologist's! Trust your own instincts in child rearing and let your neurotic tendencies mess up your kid. I don't read many parenting books written by experts. Here is why:

1. My dad said that he didn't want someone handling his finances who made less money than he did. He

had a point. Who knows what the home life of these so-called experts is like? I'm not sure I want to know.

2. I think the expression "Keep it simple, stupid" is important to remember when raising kids. I was a B–/C+ student so it's vital for the well-being of my family that I keep basic mental and physical health information very clear. I have listed some of the resources that I have used for parenting and child rearing at the end of the book. I read a few of the experts and I stick with their advice, along with my own instincts. Keeping it clear for me means—keeping it simple.

3. I think the best people to get parenting advice from are people who have great kids.

If you see a teen or young adult who is really special, sharp, and kind—ask their parents what they did. Everyone loves to talk about his or her children and this is real-life expertise based on "on-the-job training." I think these "experts" are as important or more important than someone with a bunch of letters after his or her name.

Experts: Trust but Verify

I am not an expert basher. I am just saying put your faith in yourself and your beliefs first. Read some of the books by the experts but you'll go postal if you try too many of the books. Trust in your maternal instincts and those of moms you admire and respect.

11

"Commando Is Good for You" and Other White Trash Lies You Tell Your Kids

Let's get one thing straight. Lying is wrong. But this is the White Trash guide to being a mother and I am trying to show you short-cuts for how to focus on the important things about being a mother. You want perfect, check the Martha Stewart aisle.

There are times you have to lie when you become a mom. You are forced to lie to your kids about certain things for their own good and sometimes for your own sanity.

You also must realize that there will be many occasions when your children are not telling you the truth, the whole truth, and nothing but the truth. Here is my take on the WT communication situation between parents and children.

LYING TO YOUR KIDS FOR THEIR OWN GOOD

A part of being a mother that no one tells you about is that you have to lie to your kids sometimes. In fact, it is just as much a part of motherhood as Mother's Day, apple pie, and Prozac. My mom told me some pretty big whoppers and I turned out (relatively) okay.

Here are two of the big ones I was told as a kid:

You can get pregnant through your clothes.

My mom told me that I could actually get pregnant if I made out with my boyfriend but did not go "all the way." I don't remember the exact words she used but I waited a long time to have sex because of what my mom told me. Before you write me off as a complete idiot, please note the following facts:

1. I was not the sharpest tool in the shed.
2. When I was in my teens, there was no cable, Internet, or DVDs.
3. I went to a Catholic school where one of the priests also told me this.

Your cousin is away at college.

One of the biggest whoppers that I was told as a child was that my older cousin in California was away at college. For eight years he was at college. Years later my mom told me that my cousin was really in prison. Of course, if I had Internet access back then, I could have found out that the "state college" he went to did not have an eight-year program. Please also note that I was relatively easy to lie to by parental units since I was not the "brightest bulb" around.

WHITE TRASH WHITE LIES

Word of Caution to White Trash Moms

Despite my flippant attitude you don't want to use a "tall tale" too often. Like everything else in parenting, you have to pick your battles, and you have to be selective on the number of times you utilize this WT method of sanity saving. Keep in mind that today's kids are far smarter than we ever were. Here is a three-step test that you need to give yourself before embarking on telling a lie to your savvy, streetwise youngsters:

Step One—What Is the Tale?

Example from my life: *You'll catch a cold if you don't wear a sweater!* This is a standard from the mom handbook. Children don't catch colds if they don't wear a jacket or sweater on a chilly day.

Step Two—The Reason for the Tale?

When my girls were small, they would dress themselves in outfits that were not appropriate for the weather. For example, my younger daughter went through a bathing-suit phase. You can't wear a bathing suit in December in the Midwest all the time. I had to constantly remind her to wear clothes that fit the weather. As a younger child, this daughter would wear shorts and tank tops all year long if I didn't throw a little mom guilt her way.

Step Three—Does the Benefit Outweigh the Tale?

I used to tell the "wear a sweater or catch a cold" tale when my daughter was younger because she was not at an age I could reason with her about it. Since this daughter is now almost ten years old, she understands that if she wears a tank top in December, she'll freeze.

Before you get on your high horse about lying to kids, let's take a look at the biggest, seasonal lies we tell . . .

SANTA, THE TOOTH FAIRY,
AND THE EASTER BUNNY

When you really think about the whole Santa/Tooth Fairy/Easter Bunny trifecta, it's actually pretty twisted.

- ❖ A man sneaks into your house by coming down your chimney in the middle of the night and leaves presents.
- ❖ A creature flies into a kid's bedroom at night and leaves money for teeth.
- ❖ A giant bunny leaves candy for children.

How weird are all of the above? Yet they are part of the culture in which we live. We tell the lies to keep a little magic in our lives. I quit believing in Santa when I was twenty-seven. In my family, we lived by the saying: If you don't believe, you don't receive.

Since I was a materialistic little thing, I believed in Santa for as long as I could get away with it.

MOM TALES 101

Fluffy went to my cousin Susie's farm.

I challenge any mother to tell me that they have never used the "farm" tale about a pet. If you say you haven't done this, you are either perfect or you are lying your White Trash butt off. The tale of "Fluffy to the farm" goes like this. Usually the "Fluffy" tale is due to an animal homicide. Like the time the dog ate Fluffy the cute little hamster as an appetizer.

You don't want to tell the kids that their beloved family dog ate another member of the family—Fluffy the hamster—because the kids would hate the dog. The dog was just doing what dogs do, which is to chase smaller animals . . . and Fluffy just happened to be in the wrong place at the wrong time.

So you invent "the farm." When your child comes home from school and asks, "Where's Fluffy?" you say, "Fluffy needed to be with other hamsters his age, so we had to take him to Susie's farm." Fluffy was not a snack—he was given to Susie, so he would be happier on her farm.

The *key* to having your kids believe the "farm" tale is that you need to remove Fluffy the hamster's cage, favorite toy, and food items from your home *before* your child gets home from school. Even the smallest children will be suspicious if Fluffy is gone but all his favorite hamster toys are still at the house! Take the cage and the toys to your nearest WT neighbor's house—get it out of sight immediately. Don't throw the cage and all of Fluffy's toys away though. Because the best cure for a hamster that has gone to the farm is . . . another hamster.

Eating in the car is bad for you.

One of my WT friends has convinced her four children that it is not sanitary to eat in the car. Is this crazy? Yes and no.

Yes, it is crazy from the standpoint that it is simply not true. No, it is *not* crazy because my friend's car does not smell like fast food, nor is it filled with wrappers and food stains. Crazy like a fox, my friend.

Chuck E. Cheese is only open for birthdays.

This isn't mine. It's from my friend and fellow author Devra Renner.

"I never let my son know you could go to Rat Palace (AKA Chuck E. Cheese) at other times than birthday parties. For years the kid had no idea it was a restaurant and not just a place to have a birthday celebration. Did we ever go when it wasn't someone's birthday? Yes. Did I lie about it? Kinda. When we went at those times, usually it was to meet up with other parents and kids from my son's playgroup. My son would just say, 'I bet it's so-and-so's birthday and she's just too shy to have them sing, right?' and I would answer, 'That sounds logical to me.' I am baaaaaad."

TWEENS AND TEENS

The Thin Line Between Insanity and Truth

Modern preteens and teens are so sophisticated. If you try to tell them some of the whoppers that my folks told me, they can instantly Google the information and you're busted. It takes about five seconds.

Additionally, today's kids have IM, e-mail, MySpace, and a host of multimedia platforms of communication that were not invented even a few years ago.

You can't tell today's teens "tall tales" like the ones my parents told me. Let me tell you why in basic WT words: Teenagers are crazy. You can't always reason with them. Call me bad but there is something to be said for scaring a teenager in order to get them not to try something or do something. You can tell me that we need to sit down and talk about issues—and I am all for open communication about issues like drinking, sex, or drugs. Teens need to know what you think and what the facts are.

However, a little bit of fear imparted by a crazed parent can go a long way to preventing trouble. Let's walk down memory lane, shall we?

Insanity as Prevention

Does anyone remember the end of the Cold War in the 1980s? Please bear with me, there's a point here. Everyone credits Ronald Reagan with great diplomatic skill for ending the Cold

War and bringing down the Berlin Wall. But the truth is that the rest of the world feared RR because they thought he was completely insane! They figured he was just crazy enough to push the button and nuke everybody back to the Stone Age.

Was he crazed or was he smart? Depends on your politics, and I have my own opinion. But do you see where I'm going with this?

Here is an example from my teen years. When I would get way out of hand or do something really stupid, my father would get about one inch from my face and scream at me that he was going to "send me to the convent" if I did not straighten up.

I still break out in a sweat thinking about those times, as I was really scared to see my laid-back dad turn into this crazy maniac with the vein popping out of his temple. Don't let facts get in the way of a good story, as my pal Tacky Princess always says.

Fact #1—I Was Not Even Raised Catholic

Fact #2—I'm Sure My Dad Had No Freaking Idea Where a Convent for Really Bad Teen Girls Was Located

And I wasn't even that bad! My issues were talking back, staying out past curfew—nothing you could get thrown in jail for.

The facts didn't matter. I was scared to death that my dad had completely lost it and I was headed for the convent if I didn't shape up. My dad, ever the good salesman, sold me on the fact that if I pushed my parents, he would pack me off to the nuns.

Is Acting Crazy Sometimes Really Crazy?

If your kids think you might be a little bit crazy about certain issues, it might just stop them or make them pause a little before they do something really stupid or life threatening. Making them think you are a little off-balance could be the difference between your child riding with that drunk driver or calling you for a ride. I'm sure there are a million experts that say I'm wrong but putting the fear of God (or whoever) into your teen just isn't a bad thing.

THE TALES YOUR CHILDREN TELL YOU

Children are wonderful. They are blessings from above and we are lucky to have them in our lives. But kids are put on this earth to test their boundaries and push our buttons. It's their job. It's what they do best. When dealing with our blessed little darlings, we can take a cue from how Ronald Reagan dealt with the Soviet Union: "Trust but Verify."

Trust but Verify

I think this approach is excellent for parents and children. You want to trust them. You need to trust them. But you also need to verify. Why?

Because they are children. All children, no matter how "good," are going to push the limits sometimes. You must assume that they are going to lie to you and try to scam you sometimes. Watch for it and trust them but verify that they are doing what they say they are doing.

Here are a few of the many topics that I think parents need to pay special attention to and Trust but Verify.

Examples with Younger Children

Trust but Verify #1

You ask your eight-year-old girl what is taking so long in the bathroom.

She says she is "cleaning it."

Translation: She has taken nail polish and painted the ceramic tile. She also used your Bobbi Brown powder brush to clean the toilet.

Trust but Verify #2

You ask your ten-year-old what is going on in the basement.

He says he is "doing homework."

Translation: He is playing the *Madden NFL 2007* football video game and possibly watching *Skinamax* on TV.

Trust but Verify #3

You ask your kids what happened to their white dress shirts.

They answer that they "don't know."

Translation: They killed the hamsters by accident and used the shirts to wrap up the bodies and cover the evidence. You'll find the shirts and your fluffy friends next spring.

Examples with Older Kids

Trust but Verify #1

Your thirteen-year-old daughter tells you that she is spending the night at Mary's house. Mary's mom is never home and doesn't pay much attention to her daughter.

Translation: They are having a party at Mary's house and no one is home.

Trust but Verify #2

Your fifteen-year-old son says a bunch of guys are going to see the school play and then going over to Tom's house to spend the night.

Translation: Warning! Warning! A bunch of guys going to the school play? Unless your son has consistently been involved in drama or acting, this is a lie. The boys are going to a bar with their fake IDs.

Trust but Verify #3

Your sixteen-year-old daughter is invited with her friend to visit the state university for the weekend. Her friend's sister is a freshman at the school.

Translation: She is going to get drunk all weekend with a bunch of college kids.

The Stakes Are Higher

As your kids get older, the stakes become higher. Forgive my rant in the next paragraphs but I feel strongly about this subject.

Surfing the Net

It kills me that modern moms will totally trust their children and teens to surf the Internet with no supervision. These kids are up in their rooms for hours online but these moms tell me, "Tommy told me he doesn't visit chat rooms or unapproved sites." If you are not a "technical" type of person or you don't like computers, educate yourself enough so that you can check up on your kids.

Newsflash: If your preteen or teen son is surfing the Net with no supervision, he is looking at porn or something close to it! Likewise, if your daughter is away from you and your family surfing the Net unattended, you might as well just send out an engraved invitation to the perverted forty-two-year-old guy who is cruising the chat rooms looking for young girls to come on over to your house. We may be a little White Trash but we're not stupid. Know what your kids are doing online.

Mobile/IM/E-mail

Do you know who your kids are talking to or sending messages to? You need to keep tabs on who they are talking to on their cell phones, who they are sending "IMs" to, and who is on their e-mail list. It's not that you don't trust them—it's just that you don't trust them completely. If you are paying for the service, you need to have access to check what the activity is. If they balk about the invasion of privacy, then just tell them they can pay for it themselves. That usually ends the discussion. Fight this fight hard as there are tons of people who may be trying to get to your kids.

FINAL WORDS ON LYING FROM
WHITE TRASH MOM

You lie to your kids for their own good and at times for your own sanity. I think it's okay for them to think their mom is a little crazy. It keeps them guessing. They lie to you at times because they are kids. You check up on them more than is "cool" in today's modern age.

12

If the Health Department Isn't Coming, It's Clean Enough

Whether you live in a double-wide, a McMansion, or a classic colonial, in the city or country, your home is your White Trash Palace, so treat it accordingly.

WHITE TRASH MOM'S CLEANING TIPS

I'm sure it will come as no surprise that I don't enjoy housework. So I'm not really the best resource for information on how to keep your own little double-wide trailer clean. But I do know a thing or two about making it look clean or making it look like clean is one of your priorities. Consider these tips and shortcuts just another way of attacking the perfection expectation. I'd rather fight the war on perfection than battle dust bunnies any day of the week. White Trash Mom cleaning and housekeeping tips are not for every day. WTM tips are what you can use when you experience the following:

Uh-Oh Moments

For most people, but especially ADD people like me, having an uh-oh moment is a fairly routine occurrence. For those of you not familiar with this syndrome, an uh-oh moment is when you remember that it's your turn for book club and twenty-five people are coming over in four hours. Or when you remember you offered to have the entire family to your house for dinner and you live in complete squalor. White Trash Mom tips are good for those moments when you have to do six months' worth of cleaning in a few hours.

You need extra help.

"I'm on My Last Nerve and I'm at the Maximum Dosage" Moments

There are times when life gets too busy or too crazy. When super replaces normal chaos-sized chaos that makes it hard to keep your sense of humor and your perspective.

It may be a week, a month, or longer but there are times when life goes too fast and you need to cut something out. Skimp on the chores and not on your favorite reality TV show.

If You Mess with Me, You Mess with the Whole Trailerpark

Some of the ideas and tips I am giving you are for moments when you need help in a hurry or in a crisis. Pulling it out at the last minute and operating in a crisis mode are challenges faced by most mothers on a regular basis, so that's why I'm including these tips in the book. Just don't give me a lot of hell about how I don't love the baby seals or I hate the planet because of my advice. White Trash Mom's advice is supposed to be used as a Band-Aid, not a full-time solution.

Cutting Corners Can Increase Sanity

But WTM knows there are ways to cut corners during maximum insanity times in your life and I think sanity over eco-perfect is a good thing if you are raising children.

At least it's good to have *some* sanity—no mom is completely sane because children suck some of the logic/reason cells out of your brain just before birth. It's true. My neighbor Jan told me so. And she has seven kids so I don't argue with her.

Quick Cleaning Tips When You Need a Little Sanity

Products to keep handy for those uh-oh moments:

- ❖ Clorox Disinfecting Wipes
- ❖ Swiffer Mops
- ❖ Febreze

Please don't get on me about the environment. I am not suggesting you do this every day. I'm saying these are great in a pinch. You can get a bathroom clean in ten seconds with two Clorox wipes.

A Swiffer mop is easy for a smaller child to wipe a floor down with in a hurry. Febreze helps quickly to take that "Muddy Dog Paw" smell out of your carpet or upholstery without having your house smell like a hospital.

Easy Way to Do Something Nice—Paper Products

Paper products are great when you want to do something nice for a friend or family member. Illness, new babies, or a death in the family usually means the family will get lots of creamed corn and casseroles. White Trash Moms bring paper products to people in need. They save the recipient from washing dishes during a busy time and, best of all, they're very easy and cheap.

SOLUTIONS FOR THE "I'M ON MY LAST NERVE AND I'M AT THE MAXIMUM DOSE" MOMENTS

When your mom's surgery is the same week as the big field trip (which is also the same week that you have a big deadline), you need to get a little more help. These are some of my suggestions for the extra-crazy times so you can take a little stress off yourself and breathe easier.

Use Paper Plates—Mother Nature Will Forgive You

I know that as a rule it's bad to use paper plates, but there are times when you will absolutely have a mental breakdown if you have to do another load of dishes. Save yourself during those times and use the damn paper plates.

White Trash Mom loves the planet but paper plates and cups are an easy solution for a week from hell. It saves you the time and trouble of doing dishes and takes just one of the daily chores off your list.

Take-out Food Equals Sanity

Take-out food is an easy option and there are many ways you can serve healthy, well-rounded meals by picking up your food at the deli or restaurant. If I had a trust fund, this is how I would eat every night, as I am a terrible cook. Ask anyone in my family. The problem with a lot of take-out food is that it can be expensive if you do it too frequently. But a roasted chicken from the deli with a salad from the grocery-store salad bar is a good meal for your family and can be a lifesaver.

TAKE-OUT HOME COOKING

"Social Suppers" is a business in our area where you can make a bunch of meals at their store and take them home or just walk in and buy takeout. It's a lifesaver for busy times and if you don't get the "just take-out" option, you can get the meals at a very low cost, usually under twenty dollars or so. If you don't have a Social Suppers store in your area, there are other franchises just like it and they are springing up all over the place.

THE LAUNDROMAT IS YOUR FRIEND

I know there are times when the laundry piles up. I am pretty short but there have been times, no joke, when the laundry was piled up almost as tall as I am! When the laundry gets really bad, I head for the local coin laundry.

There are two ways to go at the coin laundry:

Do-It-Yourself or Do-It-for-Me

Do-it-yourself is where you take in all your clothes and just do the laundry all at once. Take five machines and just "git her done" in a two-hour time period. You can zip through the laundry in record time and fold it there—and you're done. It beats spending eight or nine hours doing it at home, especially if you have a lot of bed linens or heavy items. I like the Laundromat because it smells good; there are good magazines, and my kids love to go there. My older daughter likes the arcade games and the younger one just loves all the little sample boxes of detergent. A trip to the coin laundry will cost you under ten dollars and save you from hours of laundry duty.

Do-it-for-me is the decadent way to go and should only be used if it's a true emergency or if you are the recipient of a winning lotto ticket. It's expensive but sometimes it can be worth it to drop off some of your stuff for "Fluff and Fold" at the Laundromat.

"GOING HEADLESS"—CRISIS SURVIVAL TIPS

Everyone has weeks, months, or years in their life when you are in survival mode. If you are lucky, you don't have too many times when you have to "go headless." This phrase was coined by one of my wise friends and I love it. It means you are in survival mode and you're plowing through life and just trying to get by. Some examples of the times when "going headless" usually occurs:

When you are going through a divorce.

When you or a loved one is gravely ill.

When life has hit you from all sides—job, home, family—at once.

Tips for Those "Headless" Times

If you are in a true crisis mode in your life or there is an extended stressful situation, you need to realize one important thing: You are not going to get things done as you normally do.

The first thing you must know about being in the midst of a big whirlwind or life crisis is that you must lower your expectations and give yourself a little breathing room. Things are not normal and they won't be for a while. You have to give yourself and your family a break. Just keep going and keep moving and you will come out the other end.

Things will be "normal" again but until that day comes, you need to adjust your attitude so you don't make yourself and your family feel more stressed by holding yourself to some unrealistic standard.

After giving yourself a break and cutting your family some slack, here are my other suggestions for making your daily life a little easier during times of high stress:

Hire Help

If you can afford it at all—hire a cleaning person. Even if it's just once a month, it can make a world of difference. Is your sanity worth seventy-five dollars extra a month? If you can afford it, do it.

Ask for Help

This is one of the hardest things to do if you are in a crisis or period of high stress. You already feel out of control and admitting it to your family and friends is hard enough. Asking them to watch your kids or go to the pharmacy for you or other tasks is even harder. But do it. If you can't lean on family and friends during hellish times, when can you?

Help from a Higher Power

You are probably surprised that a person who writes *The White Trash Mom Handbook* is advocating prayer and spiritual guidance. But it is during the worst times and the darkest times that your faith can make the difference between going on and giving up. Whatever your faith or belief, I am a big advocate for keeping your spiritual side nourished, especially when you are getting pounded by the outside world.

God Produced the People Who Invented Car DVD Players and Prozac

Car DVD players and Prozac are the greatest discoveries for modern mothers, in my opinion. These two things have saved many a mom from the brink of madness. There is no stigma about having a car DVD player but there is still a stigma attached to antidepressants. There is no shame in taking a prescription drug or medicine if you are going through a rough patch. White Trash Mom thinks that God made the scientists who created the drugs that can help you cope. Ask anyone who has ever taken a prescribed medication for postpartum depression or while going through a life crisis. Prozac (and other drugs) are a miracle for most people.

DECORATING THE WHITE TRASH HOME

Your home will never look like the Pottery Barn catalog.

Never.

The reason your home will never look like the Pottery Barn catalog is because . . . it is shot in a studio with professional lighting, set designers, and a huge staff that makes it look perfect. No one will ever have a home like the catalog because *it's not real.*

If you are, in some fashion, holding on to the fantasy that you can have a perfectly appointed home and live with children, you need to wake up. Unless you have a full-time maid, butler, and perhaps a toxic cleanup specialist on your payroll, give up the fantasy, sister! Embrace the philosophy of White Trash Mom and you will be less stressed!

Drinking the Pottery Barn Kool-Aid

I drink the Kool-Aid of Pottery Barn and I am a member of the Pottery Barn club. I buy the stuff sometimes but the minute it comes into my house, it will never look anything like the store or catalog. I like the furniture they sell but I make my purchases knowing the products will not look the same in my home.

Let me give you a few examples from my own home:

My Desk from Pottery Barn

At the Pottery Barn store, the desk unit *does not have seventeen cups of coffee on it*. The desk in the catalog picture or the desk in the store does not have earmuffs from last winter, Happy Meal toys, or gum stuck to it. I could be wrong but I am pretty sure that the home-office Pottery Barn bulletin board doesn't have green boogers pasted in the corner. I did not paste the boogers there; it is still a mystery in my household, as neither of the girls will confess.

My Younger Daughter's Bedroom

At the Pottery Barn Kids store, the beautiful bedside table isn't crammed full of old Halloween and Easter candy, and the white finish of the table isn't dotted with "Sleazy Pink" nail polish. The bed set from the store was not designed to be a gateway to the Pit of Hell or whatever it is that my daughter stores under her bed. I try not to look under the bed very often. Please note that it does not matter if we spend eighteen hours cleaning the room (which we must from time to time), the room will return to its previous level of squalor in less than twenty-four hours. It can be messy in a matter of minutes if a certain crew of friends comes over.

Cool and Hip Decor—I've Tried and Failed to Decorate

Just because a magazine has a cool decorating idea doesn't mean you can have it in your house. It's hard not to covet a chic home in our consumer-driven culture and I love magazines. Sometimes, after too many cups of coffee, I even begin to believe that if I buy enough magazines, I will be able to transform my home from its present decor of White Trash Meets Pottery Barn to a home that's featured in the magazines. A home that is shiny, pretty, organized. Then I wake up because my fantasy is abruptly shattered by the girls arguing over the Xbox play station that sits in my living room, next to the spilled glass of pop, which is next to the place on the rug where the cat threw up last year.

The reason you can't have your decor too chic is because you are a mother and you have children. You can have a cool home all the time or you can have kids. Take your pick. Even the little one is a one-person wrecking crew; it's his or her job.

I am not suggesting your home can never look nice. It can actually look great for three or four hours at a time. But to be très chic and pulled together for longer than that is impossible. I have tried a few times to decorate and here's what happened:

Magnetic Paint in Kitchen

Cool idea. Paint the area behind the kitchen counter with magnetic paint. *How smart. How efficient.* We can put notes up. I even purchased magnetic words. (I saw it in one of my magazines and I did it.) Here is what happened: My kids and their friends use the magnetic words to spell naughty things. "*I like big butts.*" Not bad but not what was intended.

This *nice* phrase is one of many examples of sentences that my children create out of my wonderful magazine idea. The "big butt" sentence is seared into my memory because I noticed it on the board *after* the entire extended family had just left the First Communion brunch we hosted. I was surprised but I knew this would happen. If kids have a chance to use some kind of "potty humor," they will take it.

Chalkboard by the Front Door

I got a chalkboard to put by the front door. How chic. How smart of me. What a good way to remember things before we leave the house. I patted myself on the back for that one.

One evening I was locking up the house and I glanced at the board.

My stomach dropped to my feet as I read the wonderful and creative messages my darling offspring had written on the board:

> *Grace farted.*
> *Clare farted.*
> *I farted.*
> *OOOH!*
> *Katie is a farter.*
> *I love to fart.*
> *That felt GOOD. Ah!*

It was also illustrated! Despite threats of torture, neither of my girls would tell me if the board had the "fart art" on it when we hosted the seventh-grade parent mixer. Judging by the level of their denial, I was pretty sure that the "fart art" was in plain view of the parents at the mixer. Hey, I suppose this all just proves I'm not one of the Muffia!

CHILDREN AS CLEANING CREWS

In addition to the fact that your home is not a photo shoot, your home will never look like the catalogs and magazines because you have children. But those same children who mess the place up make for a handy home-cleaning crew.

In the pioneer days, one of the reasons parents had children was to gain extra help in the fields or farm. Kids were loved but were also used to help the family work the land and live.

One of my dear friends tells her children: *Why do you think I had you? Get to work!*

She is kidding but as a mom of five energetic kids, she makes them pitch in and help and has done this from the time they were toddlers. I was not as smart as my friend and did not do my training early like she did. Therefore, I must do my training daily or weekly; and usually I have a "boot camp" for the family just after school ends for the year.

Summer Vacation in La-La Land

At the start of every summer vacation, my girls are under the false impression that:

- ❖ They have a full-time maid for the summer (me).
- ❖ They can operate games on PlayStation 2 or watch TV all day long.
- ❖ They are entitled to nothing but fun fun fun for the next ninety days.

My behavior modification program is pretty simple. It goes something like this:

Yelling

Yell a lot about how you live in complete squalor. As you scream, use examples of how gross the house is by taking old sandwiches out from under their beds or making them look at all the dog hair in the see-through vacuum cleaner.

Make Piles

Force them to make piles of items that they have not touched in the last two years. (If they have not used it or touched it in two years, it goes in the garage sale pile.) Do not be swayed by tears for the broken Easy-Bake Oven that Grandma gave them. Use it, throw it out, or sell it at the yard sale. If it is nice enough, give it to charity.

Hard Labor

Forced outside labor. Weeding, helping plant in the garden, help with yard work.

Brainwashing

Repeat some of the things your mom used to say to you. It's a form of brainwashing that I have found works nicely to get them over the fantasy that my entire job over the vacation is to play "cruise director" for them. My favorite mantras are as follows:

- ❖ One of the reasons parents *have* children is so they will do chores! Don't believe me? Call Mrs. Smith. Ask her what her kids are doing today.
- ❖ If your attitude continues, we can just start going to 8:15 A.M. mass *every day*. I'd love it.
- ❖ Where is the phone book? I want to check into summer school for you guys if you are so bored.
- ❖ If you are that bored, perhaps you could call Great-Aunt Cassie. I'm sure her seventeen cats need some attention . . . you could spend *all day* with her. I'll get my keys.
- ❖ I am sure Susie's mother *is* a way nicer mom than me. If you would like to do *everything* Susie does, let's call Susie's mom and get the name of Susie's oboe teacher.

Usually by the second week of vacation, the shock has worn off and they are back to reality. But I do believe in having the kids pitch in with housework and chores.

Why have them if you can't put them to work?

Reality Check—What to Expect When Kids Help

Don't expect your children to be thrilled to help you clean. It just won't happen. Here are some examples of what to expect when you ask your kids to clean . . . taken from my one little double-wide.

For those of you not blessed with having a teenager living with you, here is a peek into living with one.

How to Do Chores Like a Thirteen-Year-Old

Ask the thirteen-year-old to do an extra bit of work around the house, above and beyond the daily chore list.

Step 1—First and foremost, roll your eyes and sigh heavily and loudly. Act as if you are being held against your will in a prison or enslaved in some way. *High drama.* Academy-Award type of drama.

Step 2—Attempt to argue with the parent but stop this approach just as the parent gets irritated. Get up *slowly* from your important task (talking on the phone, IM-ing friends, or watching TV) and make your way into the kitchen. Move as though you are underwater, make sure everyone knows it is a *huge* effort.

Step 3—Load the dishwasher with only the glasses and dishes that are in the sink. Load up the dishwasher and start to run the dishwasher with only five dishes in it. Act surprised and shocked when parent stops you from completing your chore.

Step 4—Joan of Arc would be proud as you act like a martyr when your parent tells you to *look around* the kitchen to pick up other dishes. Tell parent that you "didn't realize" that they wanted you to *look for other dirty dishes.* Please note that the point of all of this is to make it such a hassle for the parent to have you do this extra chore that they won't ask you again.

Step 5—*Slowly* and *painfully* fill up the dishwasher with more than the five dishes. It will appear to the outside world that you are clearly being tortured.

Step 6—The dramatic performance of this task increases the time spent on this chore to thirty minutes. After finishing this chore, *slowly* go and report to your parent that this task is done. Tell them this information as if they had asked you to kill an entire family and bury them under the front porch—the chore is that distasteful.

It is at this point that the parent will either be completely disgusted and allow the teen to go back to more "important" tasks or the members of the household will be forced to watch additional drama.

Blame Is a Part of Housework

You can't involve your children in the cleaning process without having some blame thrown into the mix. Siblings love to blame each other for various messes and some siblings have perfected this blame game into an art form. My nine-year-old daughter is very wise in the ways of the younger sibling and is quite skilled in her role as a little sister. However, I find that her greatest performance in the role of little sister is usually in the area of blaming her big sister for a mess that has blown up in our fine WT home. Dig, if you will, the step-by-step analysis of how to do it, from my daughter, the expert:

How to Blame the Mess on Your Sister Like a Nine-Year-Old

Step 1—Hear mother screaming in the basement. Hurry to the basement to get there first.

Step 2—Listen as your mother recounts, in great detail, every item, food, beverage, and video game left out in the basement. Parent's ranting usually takes a minimum of five minutes and it's best to just them go on. It makes them feel better.

Step 3—As your mother begins to interrogate you about what part of the "horrible mess from beyond hell" is yours, your facial expression becomes blank. As your mother's questions go on, your expression evolves into a blank stare as if you have never *seen* this area of the house before. It is as if you are visiting the basement from another planet *or* as if you have just awakened from a *coma*. You look around as if you have never seen this room and have no idea what she is talking about.

Step 4—Your coma/alien expression expands to your hearing. Make your mom repeat the question, as if you are having trouble making sense of what she is saying. It's hard to comprehend her questions because you are acting as though you have never stepped foot in this room before this moment.

Step 5—Deny, deny, deny.

Step 6—Present your evidence. Immediately begin to give your arguments in the case of why your sister is the one who made the mess. Exact dates, names, and photos if you have them will be presented at this time.

An example of this type of presentation: "Big sister had two friends over on February 26, 2007, for a sleepover. The two girls ate chips. There are chips on this floor now so it's very clear that Sis and her friends are the ones guilty of leaving chips on the carpet. I rest my case."

Step 7—After presentation of the facts, your mother begins to rant once again. Listen to her and make noises like "Hmm" and "I see" from time to time.

Step 8—Without admitting any guilt, offer to "clean up" your sister's mess. This stops your mother from ranting (at least for now). Your mom goes upstairs to begin the rant all over again, to your sister. You pick up a few things, let the dog eat the chips, and turn on the TV.

Note to White Trash Moms

If a mother constantly brags about how well her children clean or how helpful they are around the house, beware. The woman has probably hired actors to pretend they are her children. No child, no matter how "good," likes housework.

13

Boring Summer Vacations
(and Other Ways I Deprive My Kids)

Apparently I missed the essential parenting memo. In case you did too, it went something like this:

Your kids are missing out on a fulfilling and complete childhood if you don't take them to Disneyland (or another really cool place) before they are eighteen.

I think in this same memo (which I missed), it also stated:

You are required to enroll your children in a hundred different summer enrichment programs and make sure they are entertained at all times when they are out of school.

There Is No "Break" from Perfection . . . Even in Summer

There is pressure, even when school is out, for kids to perform.

By today's standards, my parents deprived me of a normal

childhood because my summer schedules were a virtual waste-land.

"You need to do the advanced math over the summer with a special tutor if you want your daughter to perform well on the high school entrance exams."

"The kids that do the Hot Shot Soccer camp in June are the ones who are asked to try out for the premier team in the fall. It's almost full!"

If kids can't get downtime in childhood . . . they will never get the chance. Are there any other times besides childhood when there is a two- to three-month break from the routine? That's why I let my kids do some activities, but part of the fun of summer is relaxing from the routine.

There Is No Summer Break from the Muffia

Like death and taxes, you can count on the fact there will be Muffia. The Muffia turn the wonderful summer days into another chance to compete in the "race" to be perfect. Summer sports teams and camps are another way to use motherhood as a spectator sport.

I love the unstructured time in the summer and I love the break that it gives the girls (and me) from the Muffia. So when one of the Muffia tries to slither into our lives during the precious summer months, I try to do what I can to stop it.

It can be hard to spot the Muffia during the summer months but read and learn, White Trash Moms, so you'll know what to look for.

Our little neighborhood pool and tennis place is kind of a throwback. It's hidden in a neighborhood not far from mine and it's awesome. It is not expensive, anyone can join, and it's relaxing to hang out there. It is kind of a haven for other WT moms and WT families.

One summer our little WT haven was invaded by . . . the Muffia. I usually don't mind just one Muffia member but like mice, the Muffia tend to gather in groups. Here is how I knew she was the enemy:

Number-One Sign

She was extremely obsessed with the *ranking* of each player on the tennis team. She asked ten questions about this at the parent meeting to kick off the season.

Number-Two Sign

The mom watched a few of the girls play a match after the meeting and then when the games were over she immediately went up to several of the moms and tried to arrange a "challenge match" for her precious daughter.

Note: The challenge matches are played to determine *rank/skill level*. She only asked the moms of the younger kids and less-skilled kids.
Second Note: The rules of the tennis league indicate that the children who play are supposed to set up their own matches. A good way to usually spot a Muffia mom is that she is doing more for her kid than she is supposed to.

Number-Three Sign

A few of the moms were talking while kids were playing. This mom was very horrified to tell us that she . . . *worked part time*. Kind of like it was a disease. My WT pals and I chimed in that, yeah, we worked too; I used to work but I don't right now. It's kind of a fact of life in my world, not a chronic disease to be ashamed of. I was 90 percent sure she was Muffia after that comment.

Number-Four Sign

At the first tournament of the season, I went along to watch. The daughter of the Muffia spy kept asking the scorekeeper mom about *ranking*. After listening to the daughter ask endless questions about *rank*, this sealed it for me. I knew that a Muffia member had entered our little WT oasis of sanity.

I am not against being competitive. It is the obsession with making all things a competition that is the difference between the Muffia and the White Trash Moms.

Note: The Muffia mom ended up leaving our WT summer haven after that year. We tried to turn her but she didn't think our neighborhood pool had the "right stuff."

White Trash Mom's Guide to Summer Enrichment (or How I Deprive My Children of a Decent Childhood)

Making sure kids are entertained *at all times* when school is out is a high priority for the Muffia and those of their ilk. It's as if they think boredom for children is like a terminal disease we must wipe from the planet.

I realize that the days of taking off on a bike and messing around with friends are not something that happens anymore. There is more danger in the world than there was when I was kid. Also, more households have both parents working. Therefore, structured camps and classes can be a necessity for some families.

My kids do some things over the summer so that their brains don't turn to mush. They do some sports and swimming. But school is so filled with pressure and schedules and work—it is a grind for me so I can only imagine how they feel. I believe in giving kids some unstructured time in the summer. I know that parents who are not home need to have somewhere to send their kids when school is out, but think about letting them do something fun, so they'll feel like they are getting a break from school and schedules.

Summer Enrichment the White Trash Mom Way

Here are a few summer enrichment ideas from my childhood as well as stuff my kids do when they think I am not looking:

- ❖ Play Ding-Dong Ditch with the neighbors every day until your parents and neighbors are mad enough to spit.
- ❖ Pitch a tent in the backyard and take out all camping gear for the tent. Stay in tent five minutes. Go back inside the house.
- ❖ Spy on older siblings. Record in your near photographic memory everything they say and report in detail to your mom.
- ❖ Blackmail older siblings into giving you money for not telling what you heard during your surveillance session.

❖ Tell the bratty kid two doors down that it's polite to say s—— instead of *please* at the dinner table.
❖ Get grounded when the bratty kid two doors down actually does it and his parents call to complain.
❖ Listen in on your mom's phone conversation and repeat in detail to neighbors at the block party.

Summer Enrichment for Older Kids (Twelve and Up)

❖ Babysit the toddler kids down the street so you can read Mrs. Toddler's dirty books. Tell all your friends about it.
❖ When Mom is gone, get R-rated movies on demand. When the cable bill comes, deny, deny, deny.
❖ Hassle your parents to let you go to the new horror flick with your buddies. Act cool but lose sleep for three nights afterward because it was so scary.

WHITE TRASH MOM'S GUIDE
TO FAMILY VACATIONS

We like to travel. We do it a lot. You can find information in books like *Family-Friendly Hotels in Rome* or *See South America with Kids*. But it seems like there is an expectation that all kids have a God-given right to go to Disneyland or to an exotic beach in order to have a "real" vacation. We've taken our kids to exotic places. We've also taken our kids on road trips. It seems to me that as long as we traveled somewhere, and they weren't sleeping in their own beds, and Mom wasn't cooking—they were happy!

I am going to save you thousands of dollars in travel fees by telling you a WTM fact: *You don't have to take your kids somewhere unusual for them to have a great vacation.* You can make all the arguments you want for "enriching" them with historic or cultural vacations. You can tell yourself that you want them to see the world and that in order for them to have a good vacation, you need to spend a ton of money. Aside from giving them nothing to look forward to when they grow up, this way of thinking is dead wrong.

Three Zoos in Three Days

Two years ago, we did a long weekend tour of nearby city zoos. We visited one zoo per day and saw three zoos in three days. We stayed at budget motels and ate at cheesy roadside places . . . and the kids *loved* it. My husband and I also enjoyed it because we were relaxed and not worried about spending too much money.

White Trash Mom's Requirements for Family Lodging

Under Thirteen, Over Thirteen Rule

If your kids are under thirteen, it does not matter where you stay as long as there are a few of the critical "must haves" for vacation fun. If your kids are over the age of thirteen, no matter where you take them, they won't be impressed and no matter how hard you try, they are probably going to think you're a dork. So if the kids are over thirteen, go where *you* want to go!

Is There an Ice Machine Nearby?

Getting ice from the hotel ice machine represents some kind of tribal ritual to your children . . . even teens will get in on the act. It doesn't matter that they can go to the fridge and get ice at home. At a hotel, getting ice is the first thing they will want to do. The "ice machine race" starts less than five seconds after you enter the hotel room and continues every hour on the hour until you scream at them to go to bed.

Is There a Pool?

It doesn't matter if it is a nasty, dirty pool. It doesn't matter if you have one in your backyard at home. An out-of-town pool holds some kind of magic for children. A dank, indoor pool in a no-name motel rates the same as the beachside hotel in Cancun. A pool means superior lodgings.

Is There a Vending Machine?

It doesn't matter if the machine has two-year-old fossilized candy bars. The hotel-vending machines are magic. Again, the ritual of going to the vending machine is an hourly trip, with lots of bickering included.

Pay-per-view Movies?

It does not matter that we have more than three hundred channels at home, including fifteen movie channels. Seeing a movie on pay-per-view at the hotel makes the movie much more fun. It also does not matter if they have *seen* the movie countless times. Getting in a bed in a hotel with candy from the vending machine and watching a movie on pay-per-view is out of this world to kids.

Is There an Elevator to Argue Over?

I was in an elevator at a hotel recently. A mother and her two children walked into the elevator. They spoke Spanish but because I am fluent in Mother-and-Kid, I knew exactly what was going on. The kids were fighting over who got to push the elevator buttons. The younger kid "called" pushing the inside buttons, while the older one pushed the outside button while they were waiting for the elevator.

The older one, naturally, then rushed ahead of the younger one and pushed all of the elevator floor buttons, causing great chaos and cries of wrongdoing.

The mother was doing the "gritted teeth" smile while talking very fast and very quietly to her kids. The "Mother Giving Orders Through Gritted Teeth" is timeless and worldwide.

Good Luggage Carts for Racing?

My husband (Mr. Fun) introduced our girls to luggage-cart races. Once we were at a pretty nice resort and I had to go to the concierge, leaving hubby and kids to their own devices. When I returned to our floor, the elevator opened in time to see a luggage cart carrying Kate (who was five at the time) whizzing by at light speed. I stepped out of the elevator and narrowly missed getting run over by another luggage cart carrying our other daughter, Grace. And who do you suppose was *pushing* these luggage carts? Of course . . . Daddy.

As the carts crashed into each other, my girls fell to the

ground laughing hysterically. This cart-racing ritual takes place at every hotel/motel we stay at, much to the dismay of the management.

Is There a Game Arcade?

If there is a game arcade with gross and violent games at $5.00 a game, children are in heaven.

Make the Vacation Fit Your Family

The main point here is that the hotel could be in the next town or a faraway country, and it wouldn't make much difference to the kids as long as all the kid-friendly amenities are in place. Make the vacation fit your family values and have fun. Here are some key differences between a typical WT family vacation and a "normal" family trip:

"NORMAL" FAMILY VACATION	WHITE TRASH FAMILY VACATION
Theme park for a week	Vegas for a week
Kids get picture with Elvis impersonator	Kids get picture with Mickey
Souvenir is a tennis visor from hotel	Souvenir is poker chip holder from hotel
Kids see exotic wildlife at the wild animal park	Kids ride the elevator with two hookers

Less Stress Means Happier Vacations

Bottom line is that stressing out about a family vacation is a waste of energy and can be a waste of hard-earned money. You can take the cool and exotic vacations, but remember that you are dealing with children and teens, so your idea of a fabulous vacation spot might not match theirs.

Here's an example from my own life: My parents took the family to the Hotel del Coronado, in San Diego, when I was about ten. The "Hotel del" is heavenly and sits right on the ocean. I told my folks I didn't like it because it did not have "an indoor pool like the Holidome and it didn't have an arcade." Do you know what my parents did the next time they wanted to take a vacation? They left the kids at home and went to Mexico. They gave us money for the local arcade and left us with my old babysitter Mrs. "B," who called me *Cathy*, my brother Mark, *Mike* and my dog "Spooky," *Spikey*.

However, I was a happy ten-year-old because I had coins for the arcade and got to stay up late and watch TV with the sitter.

14

At the End
of the Day

DON'T HAVE TO BE RICH, FAMOUS,
OR CONTROVERSIAL

You don't have to be a movie star or a famous political figure to be a White Trash Mom. There are strong women all around you who are incredible. If you let go of what "perfect" is and you quit trying to be "perfect" you can be the best you can be. *Just being you is enough.*

White Trash Moms come in all shapes, sizes, and colors. The thing that makes you what I like to call a WT Mom is that you take what life throws at you and you throw it right back. You might not look like a "rebel" on the outside but it's what is on the inside that counts.

Your job as a mom is to help your kids grow into healthy and happy adults. Being a mother is extremely important.

Your job performance impacts the entire life of another human being. No pressure.

As you craft your own philosophy to fight the pressures of perfection, here are a few last words of White Trash Mom advice.

1. *Keep your sense of humor.*
   For example, if someone told you years ago: You will not be able to go to the bathroom by yourself without interruption for over twenty years and going to get dog food will be the social high point of your week, you would have laughed! How insane! How could that be? And yet it happens. The craziest part of it all is that you wouldn't trade being a mom for anything.

2. *You have kids for only a short time in your life.*
   You'll have plenty of time to dust the furniture; you'll be able to make perfect meals for years to come. You can spend the majority of your life chasing career and personal goals. But you only get a short window to be your kids' mom. Try to make it count.

3. *Create ways to work around the insanity.*
   Figure out a way to live within the rules of today and play the hand you're dealt. Spend as little of the present with the "have-to" part of life and make more time for your family. Don't worry if your solution is a little on the crazy side! The expectations placed on modern moms are crazy! Fight fire with fire.

4. *It's always five o'clock somewhere.*
   On those days when you mess up at work, the school calls to tell you there is a negative balance in

your kid's lunch account, and you feel like a failure; remember that it's always five o'clock somewhere. It's a good idea to kick back and laugh with a few friends over a coffee or a glass of wine. If this glass of wine comes at two in the afternoon, sometimes this is okay. I'm not saying to drink a martini for breakfast . . . just remember that taking a break when you need it can do wonders for your mental state.

The White Trash Mom's Hall of Fame

Remember that being White Trash is all about being who you are and not giving into the pressures of what other people think. It is about empowering yourself to do what you think is right in terms of parenting your kids and raising your family. This is my list of "Hall of Fame" White Trash Moms. This list is made up of famous women because you don't know my aunts or my sister or my sister-in-law. The women on this list are strong and they do things a little differently than the rest of the pack. I admire how they have remained true to themselves and their families. Remember, WT isn't a trailerpark, it's a state of mind.

ERMA BOMBECK (AKA THE QUEEN)

Erma took the everyday lives of women and let them know it was okay not to be perfect. Erma is the queen of writing funny and powerful words that describe being a mother. Her books and columns empowered mothers everywhere. Her work has stood up to the test of time.

Erma Bombeck's *Motherhood: The Second Oldest Profession* can crack me up any time.

ANNA QUINDLEN
One of my favorite writers, she writes great fiction about taboo subjects such as wife abuse. She also writes pointed political and social commentary in national newspapers and magazines. But she inspires me the most when she writes about being a mother and comments on some of the insanity of today's modern motherhood. She's written so much great stuff that it's hard to pick a favorite. But her book *A Short Guide to a Happy Life* is on my desk every day. If you are in a bad mood about your recent vacation to the beach or a high bill from the dry cleaner, this book is an instant reality check.

BARBARA BUSH
I want her on my side if I ever get in a fight. She's classy and plays the role of the political wife very well. But there are many examples of times she broke the rules and disagreed with her husband. She is not someone you should cross—ever.

BARBARA WALTERS
She was a high-profile working mother when no one else was doing it. Can you imagine how alone she was at the mother-daughter parties? I'm sure it was brutal raising a family with her career. Barbara Walters will not like being placed on White Trash Mom's Hall of Fame list. But if she looks beyond the trashy title, she will understand the philosophy behind the goofy White Trash Mom name. Barbara is a working mother's rock star.

BETTY FORD

Betty Ford was an alcoholic in the day when it could ruin your reputation and life. Not only did she tell the world about her problems . . . she started the Betty Ford Center to help other others with their problems. She has guts and the courage of her convictions. She was WT when WT wasn't cool.

CARRIE FISHER

Postcards from the Edge by Carrie Fisher is one of the best books ever published. *Ever.* I love her writing and her self-effacing humor. Anybody who writes like she does has to be a WTM. She's awesome and I would love to spend thirty minutes with her.

DEBBIE REYNOLDS

Nothing on the surface of Debbie Reynolds says White Trash Mom. Call it a hunch but I'm convinced she's a member of the White Trash Mom club.

FLORENCE HENDERSON

Florence played Mrs. Brady in the seventies and will always be the mom of the Brady clan to my generation. But she gets on my list because of what she has done *after* the Brady Bunch. Her self-effacing humor and her appearances on comedy TV shows makes her *awesome*. Her thirty-second part in the very black cult comedy movie *Shakes the Clown* puts her in the Hall of Fame. Florence helped put the "fun" back in "dysfunctional" motherhood.

DEMI MOORE

She's a movie star who lived the dream and then she changed her vision of the dream. She's had fame and marriage to Bruce

Willis. Then a few years off with the kids and she comes back to Hollywood with a sex-kitten body. Call it another hunch but I think she definitely is a cool and hip WTM.

Bonus points for Demi Moore: She and her ex-husband have a great postdivorce relationship.

Double bonus for Demi Moore: Marries younger guy, very happy in new marriage.

HEATHER LOCKLEAR

This actress is over forty and fabulous. She went through a divorce and her ex-husband started dating her ex–best friend. Heather Locklear just looks like she'd be fun to go and have a margarita with. Tell me I'm wrong. When I read or watch interviews of Heather Locklear, she seems self-effacing with a great sense of humor.

HILLARY CLINTON

I disagree with Hillary Clinton on several issues. I admire her and put her in the Hall of Fame because:

* She's brilliant and makes no apologies for her smarts or her ambition.
* Bill cheated on her and she stuck by him.
* The Republicans thought she'd be the anti-Christ in the Senate but she's proved everyone wrong and won the respect of many of her critics.
* Hillary doesn't give in to the pressures of whom people think she should be. She is who she is.
* She has tried to protect her daughter from the spotlight against impossible odds.

KELLY RIPA

She's done soap operas, sitcom TV, and now she sits as the diva of morning talk shows as the cohost of *Live with Regis and Kelly*. She's had her kids on the show and worn pajamas on national TV. Kelly just looks like she would be fun, as well as a good mom to have on your side in a fight with the Muffia. Kelly might look like one of the Muffia but I'm certain she's all WT Mom inside.

KIRSTIE ALLEY

She was famous and then she gained a bunch of weight. Then she lost all the weight via an ad campaign on national TV. Then she went on *Oprah* in a bikini. That takes guts and a healthy dose of self-confidence.

Bonus points for Kirstie Alley: She is from my hometown of Wichita, Kansas. She is the star of my all-time favorite movie ever made: *Drop Dead Gorgeous*. She seems like she would be a lot of fun at happy hour. My WT psychic intuition senses this about Kirstie.

J. K. ROWLING

A single mom is broke and starts writing a book about a boy wizard.

A few years later J. K. Rowling has given millions of children and adults a classic story that will live for years to come. Something tells me J. K. would be fun at a party, but even if she's not, she's on my list.

MADONNA

She danced in pointy bras and annoyed the Catholic Church in the 1980s and is now a mom of two kids, a writer, and her career is still going strong. Love her or hate her, she is proud of who she is and is constantly reinventing herself with no apologies. Madonna rocks in many ways and I will be listening to Madonna until I am barking in my oatmeal at the nursing home.

Bonus points for Madge: I think she is the WT Mom who has some of the best stories and would be fun to go out with. Face it, anybody with the moxie to change her name to "Madonna" has to have *great* stories.

MARIA SHRIVER

She is a great writer, maverick, and WT Mom. A member of the Kennedy family, she married the super Republican weight lifter. I'll bet that went over like a lead balloon the first time she brought Arnold home. She has had a broadcast career and is now a mom, author, as well as wife/chief adviser to the governor of California. She could send in *The Terminator* in a fight with the Muffia.

MARGARET THATCHER

As the controversial prime minister of the United Kingdom in the 1980s, she was a rule breaker and changed the political landscape. One of my favorite quotes from Mrs. Thatcher: *If you want something said, ask a man. If you want something done . . . ask a woman.* You might disagree with her political views but she called it as she saw it.

NICOLE KIDMAN

Incredible actress who came into her own after a public divorce from Tom Cruise. Extremely classy and never dished the dirt on Tom Cruise to the media. Nicole gets the last laugh as she continues to expand her star quality and raise a family.

ROSIE O'DONNELL

Rosie tells the world she's a lesbian, fights for the rights of children and families, and has been a pioneer for same-sex marriage and family. She's controversial but she is true to herself and has used her fame to pave the road for others. I don't advise her brand of open commentary at the PTA meeting because your kids will pay for it. But I give her snaps for saying what she thinks and letting the chips fall.

SUZANNE SOMERS

Played a ditzy blond on a popular TV show, then became an author, official spokesperson for the ThighMaster infomercials, and made buckets of cash selling her own brand of products on Home Shopping Network. Suzanne is the rock star of White Trash motherhood.

"HONORARY MOMS" FOR WHITE TRASH
MOM'S HALL OF FAME

DOLLY PARTON

She is a Country and Western icon who has earned the respect of the "mainstream." She makes no excuses for her blond hair, long nails, or large chest. She never gave birth to a child but she's inspired so many women just by being herself. She sings like an angel and Dolly is the reason that many people tried to listen to Country music. Her innovations in music are why she's on my list of "honorary" White Trash Moms.

OPRAH

She's not a mother. She's not trashy. But remember, a White Trash Mom is about being who you are and not giving in to the pressures of what other people think.

Oprah has done so much to empower so many women and has broken barriers so she gets a place on my own personal Hall of Fame. She came from a tough childhood to build a media empire and become one of the most successful women in the world. For those of you who say Oprah isn't a mother—too bad. If you think I am just sucking up to Oprah, kiss my trashy butt.

MOMS I WANT TO DO PLAYGROUND DUTY WITH

These women have what it takes to be a WT Mom. Here are some people that I am watching for future induction into my Hall of Fame.

ARIANNA HUFFINGTON

Huffington went from being a hard-core right-winger to a huge voice for moderate and liberal political views via the *Huffington Post*. As the founder of the online news and aggregated blog, she is consistently in the news for taking on big issues and powerful people without fear.

MARTHA STEWART

Yes, Martha Stewart.

Martha has fed the myth of perfection and created the benchmarks for Muffia mothers everywhere. But Martha fell from grace, went to prison, and came back stronger than ever. Her resilience is the reason I'm considering her for a place in the Hall of Fame.

Bonus points for Martha Stewart: Her media and products suck money out of the wallets of the evil Muffia on a daily basis. I have a soft spot in my heart for this reason alone.

CATHERINE MARGUERITE JONES (1929–2000)

Finally, this section would not be complete with a reference to one of the greatest people that you will *never* know: my mom.

My mom was an extremely classy lady with a wicked sense of humor. I didn't realize how great her sense of humor was until I was older. My mom, like many others of her generation, felt like they had to present a certain side of themselves to their children. It wasn't until I was an adult that I truly appreciated her.

My mom wouldn't like being called a White Trash Mom. She would like it if I told her I thought she was a White Trash Mom because she was strong and didn't let people push her around.

Mom played the game to a certain point. But anyone who underestimated her quiet nature and her wonderful manners was in for a surprise. The woman was like a freight train. Mom was always pulled together and well groomed, very nice and polite to everyone she met. However, she had very particular ideas of how things should be done and was very strong in her opinions.

Cancer and Khaki Pants

My mom was diagnosed with cancer when I was pregnant with Katie, my youngest daughter. They gave her three months to live. She ignored them and lived for a few years, until after my daughter's second birthday and then some. In the last few weeks before she died, she was forced to be on an oxygen tank. My mom was in the late and final stages of breast cancer. It was actually breast, lung, and abdomen cancer. My brother took her to doctors who would only tell him that "she should have died two years ago." My brother wasn't surprised, as he had experienced her force of will his entire life.

I was staying with Mom for a few days the week before she died. I was not fazed in the least that she continued to go about her daily routine. Every day, even at the very end of her life, she wore makeup and perfume. She dressed in nice pants and a shirt as if she was ready to go to lunch with a friend . . . even though she couldn't leave the house because of the oxygen tank. She may have been dying but her toenails were manicured, her lipstick was on, and at age seventy she was preparing her taxes for the CPA (despite the fact she was probably not going to live to file that year).

As if it were just another visit, Mom sent me on some errands. She wanted me to exchange some pants to the local department store (she wanted another color). When I got in my car to run her errand, I called my sister and asked: *"Where is she going to wear these pants? Why does she bother?"*

I wasn't being unkind or mean. I was just amazed by my mom's will and ability to plow through bad times. Her skills of denial were also very impressive.

My sister (who had always been smarter than I was) reminded me that our mom was dying but she was still *our mom*. Her force of will was legendary in our family and my sister reminded me that Mom was facing death as she did her life. Mom put on her lipstick and her game face, whatever the circumstances. She just kept going.

I did what I was told and exchanged the pants. However, true to form, my mom was extremely miffed at me when I showed her the new pants because: "Those pants are bone not khaki, Michelle! I wanted khaki pants." After a short lecture on the huge differences between the color bone and the color khaki, Mom sent me back to the department store. She was not going to let cancer or her daughter's ignorance of the color khaki stop her or change her routine in any way.

Mom stood for all of the stuff that the "feminist" movement meant but she did it in her own way. She didn't burn any bras but she did what she could to bust through and live life on her own terms, for the good of her family.

She was amazing and I miss her every single day.

But she taught me well and I've had the good fortune to be surrounded by a number of great women who have encouraged me to not accept the status quo. If you don't like something, try to change it. If you can't change it, work around it. If you can't work around it, laugh about it.

Life is what you make of it. You decide if you make it chicken shit . . . or chicken salad.
—*Murl Sherrod Jones (1920–92)*

I was also lucky to have an amazing dad.

APPENDIX B

The White Trash Mom's Bookshelf

Here are books to support you in your newly discovered White Trash Mom's philosophy of motherhood.

BOOKS BY OTHER WHITE TRASH MOMS

These mothers might not call themselves White Trash Moms but their books contain advice, humor, and some great drink recipes.

Bort, Julie, Aviva Pflock, and Devra Renner. *Mommy Guilt: Learn to Worry Less, Focus on What Matters Most, and Raise Happier Kids.* New York: AMACOM, 2005.

Mead-Ferro, Muffy. *Confessions of a Slacker Mom.* Cambridge, MA: Da Capo Lifelong Books, 2004.

Mellor, Christie. *The Three-Martini Playdate: A Practical Guide to Happy Parenting.* San Francisco: Chronicle Books, 2004.

Pearson, Allison. *I Don't Know How She Does It.* New York: Anchor, 2003.

Roberts, Melinda. *Mommy Confidential: Adventures from the Underbelly of Motherhood.* San Diego, CA: Aventine Press, 2006.

Wilder-Taylor, Stefanie. *Naptime Is the New Happy Hour (and Other Ways Toddlers Turn Your Life Upside Down).* New York: Simon Spotlight Entertainment, 2008.

———. *Sippy Cups Are Not for Chardonnay (and Other Things I Had to Learn as a New Mom).* New York: Simon Spotlight Entertainment, 2006.

EXPERTS YOU NEED TO READ

I have bashed books written by "experts" but there are a few books that are mandatory reading. Do not pass go. Do not collect two hundred dollars. Go and get these books *now*.

Understanding Cliques, Talking to Other Parents

Wiseman, Rosalind. *Queen Bee Moms and Kingpin Dads.* New York: Three Rivers Press, 2007.

———. *Queen Bees and Wannabes.* New York: Three Rivers Press, 2003.

Great Resources on Parenting and Life

Abrahamson, Eric, and David H. Freedman. *A Perfect Mess: The Hidden Benefits of Disorder.* New York: Little, Brown and Company, 2007.

De Becker, Gavin. *Protecting the Gift*. New York: Dell, 2000.

Lavoie, Richard. *It's So Much Work to Be Your Friend*. New York: Touchstone, 2006.

Understanding Modern Motherhood

Bombeck, Erma. *Motherhood: The Second Oldest Profession*. New York: Dell, 1987.

Quindlen, Anna. *A Short Guide to a Happy Life*. New York: Random House, 2000.

Warner, Judith. *Perfect Madness: Motherhood in the Age of Anxiety*. New York: Riverhead Trade, 2006.

APPENDIX C

The White Trash Mom
at the Movies

Drop Dead Gorgeous
The 40-Year-Old Virgin
Hairspray
Heathers
Knocked Up
Legally Blonde
Little Miss Sunshine
Mean Girls
Napoleon Dynamite
Office Space (the neighbor with the mullet is priceless)
Orange County
Postcards from the Edge
Raising Arizona
Running with Scissors
Strangers with Candy
Talladega Nights: The Ballad of Ricky Bobby

There's Something About Mary
Vacation
Waitress
Wayne's World
Wedding Crashers

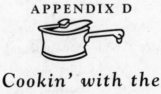

Cookin' with the White Trash Mom

The best part about these recipes is that they are easy to make. If a recipe is hard, I could not do it. I am that bad a cook. These recipes will bring you tons of fun and enjoyment and are a great addition to any gathering.

White Trash Gingerbread Double-Wide

A festive and trashy way to make a gingerbread house. This recipe uses graham crackers, and at the end you have a double-wide trailer instead of a boring Swiss Miss–type of house.

2 cans vanilla frosting (8-oz. cans)
1 box sugar cubes (1-lb. box)
2 boxes graham crackers (15-oz. box)

¾ *cup granulated sugar*
1 *16-oz. bag Skittles*
1 *10-oz. box Jujubes (or other colored candy)*

STEP 1. BUILDING THE BASE

Spread a thick coat of frosting out on flat platter or cookie sheet. Make the foundation for the trailer using the sugar cubes. Place the sugar cubes in the frosting, making a small "square" for the graham crackers to stand against. Use 5 cubes for each side of the square. Frost the cracker edges and stick crackers lengthwise on each side of the sugar cube foundation. Use frosting to "glue" each corner together. Let foundation sit for 30 minutes in the refrigerator. Take out and begin step 2.

STEP 2. FINISH THE MASTERPIECE

Frost two more graham crackers on both sides. Put these frosted crackers top of the foundation, the frosting is the "glue" for the roof of the double-wide. Make the frosting thick!

Sprinkle a little sugar on the "roof" of your trailer to give it that holiday look. Add Skittles around the edge of the roof for the Christmas lights. Stick Jujubes all around the Christmas Trailerpark for a touch of class. Use as many or as few as you like.

To top off this WT holiday masterpiece, put a toy "Hot Wheels" car in the front yard.

Finally, sprinkle sugar all around the trailer yard and all over the frosting for SNOW.

Here are some WT recipes to liven up your dessert table! One of the staples of WT cooking is the Hostess Twinkie. You can find variations of my Twinkie recipes via the wonderful Hostess Web site www.hostesscakes.com.

Thanksgiving Twinkie Kebobs

Just serve up some Thanksgiving Twinkie Kebobs and see your elderly Aunt Essie have a total cow! Add a little zip to your Thanksgiving din din, using one of the staples of White Trash cooking, the Hostess Twinkie.

16 Hostess Twinkies (one for each kebob)
½ cup raspberries or blueberries
30 to 40 Starburst candies or jelly beans
16 Stick/Kebob Thingys

Cut each Twinkie into four equal pieces.

Stick a Twinkie, piece of fruit, and candy on each kebob. Make your own colorful arrangement of fruits and candies.

To the severely cooking-impaired: Stick the kebob through the Twinkie, not the cream filling.

Yield: 16 Kebobs

Hostess Twinkies Sushi

When you think of Twinkies, you immediately think of Japan, right? Well, you will after you see this awesome recipe for Hostess Twinkies Sushi! Some recipes for Hostess Twinkies Sushi recommend putting dried mangoes or apricots on the plate. But I've found this is a waste of time as my family gobbles up the Hostess Twinkies Sushi instantly.

4 Hostess Twinkies
32 jelly beans, bright colors
2 Fruit Roll-Ups (use a green Fruit Roll-Up if you are going for "realism" in your dessert; if not, my kids like the multicolored roll-ups)

Slice the Twinkies into 4 pieces each. (I cut mine so that they are as big as my thumb.) About one-inch pieces are good.

Take Roll-Ups out of their wrappers, then slice them into pieces that are wide enough to go around the Twinkie you just cut.

Wrap the Fruit Roll-Ups around the pieces of Twinkie. Place the jelly beans into the Twinkie cream filling. Yum!

To serve, place the Hostess Twinkie rolls on a plate, cream and jelly bean side up.

Yield: 16 pieces of "sushi"

WT Puffballs

Make your double-wide a welcoming place for the family. Serve up some WT Puffballs.

2 8-oz. packages refrigerated crescent dinner rolls
1 8-oz. package sliced pepperoni (any brand)
1 8-oz. package cream cheese

Take out the crescent rolls, and shape each roll into an individual triangle. Slice each triangle into three small triangles. Chop each pepperoni slice into small pieces. Mix the chopped pepperoni into the cream cheese; make sure it's well blended. Take 1 teaspoon of the cream cheese-pepperoni paste and drop it into the middle of the triangles. Pinch up all of the dough around the sides of the filling. It should look like a Hershey's Kiss. Repeat for each triangle, place on a cookie sheet, and bake by following the baking instructions stated on the package of crescent rolls. Baking time for the rolls is normally 10 to 12 minutes at 350°F. Let cool on a rack or on the front porch of your trailer for a few minutes before serving!

Yield: 48 Puffballs

White Trash Sweet Snack

1 12-oz. bag butterscotch chips
1 stick (4 ounces) butter
1 cup peanut butter
1 box Rice Chex cereal
Nonstick spray
1-gallon freezer bag containing 3 cups powdered sugar

Melt the butterscotch chips, butter, and peanut butter together in your trusty microwave.

Pour the melted mixture over the cereal and stir. It helps if you use a shot of nonstick spray on the spoon or spatula you are using; it will make it easier to stir.

Mix the cereal until it is well coated with the butterscotch/peanut butter/butter mixture; pour the cereal into the gallon-sized freezer bag with the powdered sugar in it. Zip up this freezer bag tight, make sure it's closed, and shake it like crazy.

Repeat this shaking action until all of the cereal has been coated with sugar.

Put the mixture on a serving platter and cool for at least 30 minutes. Serve.

Yield: Enough for 10 servings

White Trash Wedding Cake
(Ding Dong Cake)

❖

(Note to WT Moms: This recipe is *not* one to take to school!)

2 boxes Hostess Ding Dongs
Marshmallow Fluff, as needed
Various treats or flowers, for garnish

Put six Ding Dongs on a plate. Spread a thin layer of Marshmallow Fluff on top of the Ding Dongs. Repeat this process, building a pyramid of snack-food cakes. Put fewer Ding Dongs on each layer as you build your cake higher. Use various treats or flowers to garnish your Ding Dong Cake. It's so pretty you could use it for your wedding (or your next one)!

Tangwich

Marshmallow Fluff, as needed
2 slices of bread—white bread, not wheat (Wonder Bread is best.)
Powdered Tang drink mix, as needed

Spread a thick layer of Marshmallow Fluff on one slice of bread. Sprinkle powdered Tang on the bread, covering all the Fluff. Spread a layer of Fluff on the other slice of bread. Press the two slices of bread together and you have an excellent WT meal! A delicious Tangwich. Wash the Tangwich down with a cold pop!

Yield: 1 excellent WT Sandwich

The White Trash Mom's Favorite Blogs and Web Sites

This is a list of all of my favorite Web sites in the world. Some of these sites are related to motherhood and some are just weird and wonderful. I know I am leaving people out and beg your forgiveness for not including you. I am WT, after all.

8 Centimeters Deluded: http://8centimetersdeluded .blogspot.com

A Flyover Blog: http://aflyoverblog.typepad.com

A Little Lipstick . . . : http://alittlelipstick.blogspot.com

A Whiff of Smiff: http://sharonsmiff.blogspot.com

Adventures in Stepford: http://instepford.blogspot.com

agentbedhead.com: http://agentbedhead.com

Alabama Improper: http://alabamaimproper.blogspot.com

Baby on Bored: http://babyonbored.blogspot.com

Bad Fortune Cookie: http://badfortunecookie.blogspot.com

Blogebrity: http://blogebrity.com

Blogger Chicks: http://izzymom.com

Blogging Chicks: http://bloggingchicks.blogspot.com

Blogher: www.blogher.org

BlondeMomBlog: www.blondemomblog.com

Busymom: www.busymom.net

Celebitchy: www.celebitchy.com

Crazy Lady in Vegas: www.crazyladyinvegas.com

Disney Family Bloggers: http://family.go.com

Fortyish Is Fab: www.fortyishisfab.com

Go Fug Yourself: http://gofugyourself.typepad.com

Her Bad Mother: http://badladies.blogspot.com

LDSM-Soccer Mom: http://ldsm-soccer-mom.blogspot.com

Lil Duck Duck: http://lilduckduck.com

Mamma Loves . . . : http://mammaloves.blogspot.com

Mom Gadget: http://momgadget.com

Mom-101: http://mom-101.blogspot.com

The Mommy Blog: www.themommyblog.net

Mommy Does It All . . . : http://mommydoesitall.blogspot
.com

Mommy Needs Coffee: www.mommyneedscoffee.com

Mommy off the Record: http://mommyofftherecord
.blogspot.com

Mrs. Mogul: http://mrsmogul.blogspot.com

My Left Wing: www.myleftwing.com

Not Winning Mother of the Year: http://
notwinningmotheroftheyear.blogspot.com

Of the Princess and the Pea:
http://oftheprincessandthepea.blogspot.com

Oh, the Joys: http://othejoys.blogspot.com

Pajiba: www.pajiba.com

ParentDish: www.parentdish.com

Peggy, as She Is: http://peggys-musings.blogspot.com

Plain Jane Mom: http://plainjanemom.com

Queen of Spain: http://queenofspainblog.com

Redneck Mother: http://redneckmother.blogspot.com

Rocks in My Dryer: http://rocksinmydryer.typepad.com

RockStar Mommy: www.rockstarmommy.com

Sarah and the Goon Squad: http://sarahandthegoonsquad
.com

shellis sentiments: http://shellis-sentiments.com

Slacker-moms-r-us: http://slacker-moms-r-us.blogspot.com

Slave to Target: http://slavetotarget.blogspot.com

So Cal Mom: www.socalmom.net

Suburban Turmoil: http://suburbanturmoil.blogspot.com

sweetney: www.sweetney.com

Three Kid Circus: www.threekidcircus.com/threekidcircus

Where's Mommy's Prozac?: http://annoyed-partyofone.com/

Woulda Coulda Shoulda: http://wouldashoulda.com

APPENDIX F

The White Trash Mom's Frequently Asked Questions

For those of you who are ADD or happen to be one of those people who like to read the end of the book first, here are some of the FAQs that we get from readers of the White Trash Mom blog. If you want a quick answer to some of the stuff in the book, take a look below.

What is White Trash Mom and do I have to live in a double-wide to read your blog?
White Trash Mom is just a shorthand name for the opposite of perfect. It really has nothing to do with trailerparks or funnel cakes. The name was chosen because today's standards for motherhood are way too high, and people need to be reminded that some of these standards are insane. In our modern world, perfection appears to be what is simply the status quo. Therefore, anything less than the perfect standards mean that you, as a mom, are not measuring up.

What do you mean when you say today's standards are perfect?
Perfection is in. The message to mothers is that you can have the cool career and the family and the size 0 figure. The message to all of us out there in the motherhood trenches is that *it's easy to do it all*. What nobody mentions is that the movie star who is a working mom also has a full-time nanny, a cook, a personal trainer, and a driver to help her out. Mere mortals read the articles about high-profile moms and beat themselves up over the fact that they cannot juggle the career and family with the same ease depicted in magazines and on TV. Many women know in their heads that much of the stuff they read is propaganda, but there is just so much of it that most modern moms have doubts about their inability to do it "all."

Why write a blog about it? Don't you have better things to do?
I write the blog as a way of spreading the message of reality to modern moms. As a former "six-figure" executive/mom, I had a full-time nanny, a maid, and a fairly modern husband helping me "do it all." And I about lost my mind.

I am not saying that women can't balance a family and a career. But I would just like someone to point out that it is a bit more difficult than it is made out to be in the media. I am just tired of perfectly sane and hardworking women beating themselves up for not being able to do the job of three to four adults at the same time. I know women can work outside the home and have a family. But since being a mother is a full-time job all by itself, I feel compelled to give people more of the "real" story.

The "Martha Stewart-ish" myth that women can "have it all" and that it's a piece of cake is just total fantasy. In a nutshell, it took me a few years and some great buddies to figure out that I wasn't failing because I could not be perfect. I am just trying to save some other women that head trip.

What in the hell are you talking about when you blog about the Muffia?

In every school in every city in the United States there is an unwritten code of conduct for motherhood performance. It is different in every school and town but this code of conduct is made up by a small group of mothers known as the Muffia.

This system that defines modern elementary and middle-school pecking order changes from place to place. But there is one fact that does not change, no matter where your children go to school. If you ignore the unwritten rules or rebel against the system, it is *your children*, not you, who will pay the price. Fitting into your children's school "structure" and being a team player helps your child. It might totally not fit you but this is just part of being a mom that they don't tell you about in the parenting books. That is one of the reasons I write my blog: to tell moms the truth and to help them find shortcuts around the insanity. To sum it up, you have to play the game. But you can figure out ways to do it that don't turn you into another person you don't want to be.

If I am well groomed and stylish, does that make me one of the Muffia?

No! Being well groomed or wearing nicer clothes certainly does not make you a member of the dark side. One of my best friends in the whole world is extremely fashionable and always looks pretty fabulous. However, I have known the woman since second grade and she was always like this. It's hardwired into her DNA. Being dressed nicely does not make you Muffia. Good grooming does not make you a bitch. However, judging other moms by the way they look or dress is the kind of behavior that I am talking about when I write about the Muffia. My pal who was born a snappy dresser would walk through fire for me or anyone that needed it. She would just do it looking great.

If I like to bake or cook, am I Muffia?

No, Virginia. Baking or cooking does not make you Muffia. Using baking or cooking as a way to impress other moms or to make other women feel bad is what makes you a member of the Muffia. One of my best friends in the world is a wonderful cook. She can whip up in a blink of an eye a plate of cookies that tastes like heaven. She loves to do it. She always has loved to cook. *She is not changing who she is to impress anyone.* I cannot boil water but she thinks I can do a host of other stuff that is awesome. She does not judge people by their ability to whip up a meal or make a cake. You belong to the Muffia if you judge others by their ability to bake or cook. You are Muffia if you look down on moms who order takeout more than cook at home.

Bottom Line: Being Muffia has far less to do with the outside things like how you look or how you cook. It has to do with the inside stuff like being mean to other mothers. Being Muffia is being *mean* and not being *real*. It's about keeping up a totally bogus and stupid standard of perfection that is unrealistic. It is about not supporting your fellow moms and being a snob. Hope I have made it a little clearer.

Please note that I did not think up the name "Muffia." It comes from the excellent book, *I Don't Know How She Does It* by Allison Pearson. I keep mentioning this because I want to give credit where it is due.

The White Trash Mom Glossary

Brown-nose
To flatter or "suck up" to teachers and school administrators so that they view your child in a favorable light.

Chill pill
What we all need to remind ourselves that we are just a tiny speck in this universe; helps us not take ourselves (and others) so seriously. Used in a sentence: "Bluffington's mom is going crazy with that auction program. She could use a *chill pill.*"

Club sports
Refers to kids' sports programs where, generally speaking, your child has to "try out" to even make the team. Often very expensive and potentially lasts year-round. Count on two to four practices per week plus games and/or tournaments all over town and sometimes all over the country. Pack your bags, hit the ATM, and watch out for "bleacher butt."

Commando
Refers to going without undergarments when the occasionally errant WTM doesn't get the laundry done in time for the *little monsters* to go back to school on Monday. Used in a WT sentence: "Kids, going *commando* is good for you every now and then. It just lets things air out."

Future filmmaker
Refers to the oldest daughter of White Trash Mom.

Going headless
Everyone has weeks, months, or years in her life when she is in survival mode. If she is lucky, she doesn't have too many times in her life when she has to "go headless."

Going postal
See definition for *I'm on my last nerve and I'm at the maximum dosage*. It is during a time period when you are IOMLNAIATMD that you might go postal. Going postal involves screaming at your children at full volume. Profanity is optional.

I'm on my last nerve and I'm at the maximum dosage
There are times when life gets too busy or too crazy; when normal chaos is replaced by supersized chaos.

A "JonBenét" moment
When other humans, usually the childless kind, look at you as if you are the kind of mother who would dress up your four-year-old like a hooker and participate in beauty pageants. Used in a sentence: "I had a very *JonBenét moment* when I asked the

salon stylist when my eleven-year-old could start getting high-lights."

Kick the can
I don't believe this. Did you grow up underneath a rock? Did you really have to look this one up, or are you just reading this for fun? This term refers to one of my very favorite games from childhood. It's a take on hide-and-seek, where the people hiding try to "come in free" by running toward a can (from last night's SpaghettiOs, naturally) and kicking it. If they make it before being tagged by the person who is "it," they're free. If they get tagged in the process, they're "it." As with *sardines*, this game is best played in the dark. And it was waaaaay more fun back when *everyone* didn't have fences. We usually played in six yards.

Little monsters
The term lovingly used to describe all of the precious children in the world, both one's own and those of others.

Margarita
The name my eight-year-old told everyone she wanted to have for Girl Scout camp last summer. Other girls chose names like Flower and Butterfly and Pocahontas. Not my little Miss Minnesota. She wanted to be Margarita, "'cuz my daddy said they're real good, and I can drink them someday real soon when I'm just a little bit older!" The Muffia mommies thought this was just hilarious, let me tell you . . .

Miss Minnesota
The name of my eight-year-old daughter in the White Trash Mom blog. Comes from the fact that she wanted to be *Miss Min-*

nesota for Halloween last year. So I had to find an evening gown for a seven-year-old, leading to many . . . *"JonBenét" moments* at the mall.

MMC

Term for Major Mental Case mothers. Mothers who can turn an easy gig like being a Room Mom into one hell of an assignment. MMCs have a propensity to "go crazy" on you when you least expect it, and there's absolutely nothing you can do about it.

Momisms

All the insane things that you swore you would never say as a mother . . . but then they just happen. Example: "I don't have time to go to the emergency room now so if you break a bone, you will have to wait until tomorrow to get help" or "Eat all your peas because you could be in ——— with all the starving children."

The Muffia

Short Answer—Remember the meanest girls in your seventh-grade class? Imagine that these girls are now adults and they have kids in school with your kids.

Longer answer—Mean and snobby mothers who are the adult bullies at the school your child attends. Being a part of the *Muffia* is being mean and not being real. It's about keeping up a totally bogus and stupid standard of *perfection* that is unrealistic. It is taking motherhood and making it a spectator sport.

The problem with the *Muffia* is that if others buck the system they have created and try to rebel too much, it will be your children (not you) who *pay* for the rebellion.

Please note that I did not create the name Muffia but that it comes from the excellent book *I Don't Know How She Does It* by Allison Pearson.

Oh s—— moments
Forgetting until the last minute that you have twenty-five people coming over for dinner.

Posse
Refers to the pack of women that *Muffia* hangs out with. *Muffia* meets her *posse* (all perfectly coiffed and in full makeup) at the coffee shop for those all-important meetings after drop-off in the morning. Used in a sentence: "Tiffany and Misty waved gaily at their *posse* from across the parking lot, as they sprinted over to join in the backstabbing fun."

The Queen of White Trash (AKA Queen of WT)
This is my "blog" name in the White Trash Mom blog.

Sardines
Are you kidding me? Do you really need this defined? What kind of childhood did you have? This is the game of good clean fun from yesteryear where one kid is appointed "it." "It" hides while the other *little monsters* split up and separately start searching for her. Once you find "it," you join her by squeezing into whatever space "it" has hidden in. Eventually, there will only be one person left, while all the others are crammed into one dark, sweaty, stinky spot. That one person left becomes the next "it," and you start the fun all over again. Best played in the dark.

Señor Patron
My alcoholic drink of choice. Smooth tequila that can knock you into oblivion just when you need it most. *Warning: After-effects can be lethal.*

Sports ROI (Return on Investment)
Similar to *Volunteer ROI analysis*, this refers to the perceived benefit parents get for the untold hours (and money) put in toward their children's budding sports careers. Let's see, we'll figure you spend a total of about 10 hours per week on average per budding young "athletic phenom," 52 weeks a year, with the average American family having 1.9 children each. That's 988 hours per year. Let's be conservative and figure your time at twenty-five-dollars an hour. That comes to $24,700. If only you were being paid . . . and don't forget that doesn't include all of Junior's sneakers, jockstraps, cups, and cleats. Those can really add up.

St. Timothy
Long-suffering husband of Michelle Lamar, the original White Trash Mom.

Summer enrichment
Paying a lot of money so your kids don't get bored in the summer.

Sweet spot
The combination of high visibility/low volunteer hours, which is the White Trash Mom's goal in any volunteer situation.

Tacky Princess
My partner in crime. She is the coauthor of the White Trash Mom blog, as well as a "mole" for inside the world of the *Muffia*.

Trash Talkin' Turleen
Turleen has rollers in her hair, a cig in her mouth, and is nine months pregnant. She burps and talks. I used to sell these dolls online in my store, whitetrashpalace.com. My *future filmmaker* and her friends used the doll for their movie epic *The Tales of Bobby Jo*.

Volunteer ROI (Return on Investment) analysis
This scientific-sounding term simply refers to the perceived bang or benefit one receives in relation to the countless hours one spends as a volunteer slave.

White Trash haven
Also referred to as WT haven; the term used to refer to the comfort and safety that *is* the White Trash home. Whether tastefully appointed with gnomes out front or last summer's inflatable pool out back, the *White Trash haven* is where the WTM goes to kick back and relax with a swig of *Señor Patron*, shoots the breeze with her WT man, and fixes the microwave burritos for the *little monsters*. Used in a sentence: "After the harrowing experience at the school ice cream social, I retreated to the safety of my *White Trash haven* once again."

White Trash Mom's fake cake recipe
Steps to make a store-bought cake look home-baked.

White Trash Mom's fake purse escape
Refers to White Trash Mom's method of leaving the office early in an undetected fashion. The WTM simply leaves behind her fake purse. It's also a good idea to leave on the light. A can of soda on your desk is a nice touch, as well.

White Trash Mom's imaginary client
Refers to White Trash Mom's method of using an imaginary client as a way to take children to the dentist or to do playground duty.

WTM
White Trash Moms. I won't bother with a definition here, as this entire book is devoted to the concept of White Trash motherhood. If you haven't grasped it by now, you're doomed.

The zen of the White Trash Mom
The eternal struggle for all White Trash Moms. How to blend in and be a part of the community enough to benefit your child without getting too caught up in political games that your actions impact on your child. This is the struggle and the balance you must have to be in touch with your inner WTM.

ABOUT THE AUTHORS

MICHELLE LAMAR

Michelle Lamar began the White Trash Mom rebellion against perfection in 2005. Michelle is a mother, wife, marketing consultant, writer, and geek.

She writes about her White Trash Mom philosophy daily via the White Trash Mom blog. Michelle writes a blog called "Seek the Unique" for Disney's Family.com. Michelle is married to Tim, also known as St. Timothy by those who know the couple. Michelle and Tim reside with their two daughters, along with two pugs, one Lab, and a cat. Michelle dreams about a small beach cottage where she can raise pugs, watch reality TV, and drink margaritas.

MOLLY WENDLAND

Molly (aka Tacky Princess) Wendland is a former member of the Muffia, and now works to spread the message of "nonperfection" to mothers everywhere. Molly is a professional writer, and in addition to her work on White Trash Mom, she writes a blog called "Balancing Act" for Disney's Family.com.

Molly lives with her husband, Steve, her two daughters, and a dog, who rules the household.